RC Formula1 .com

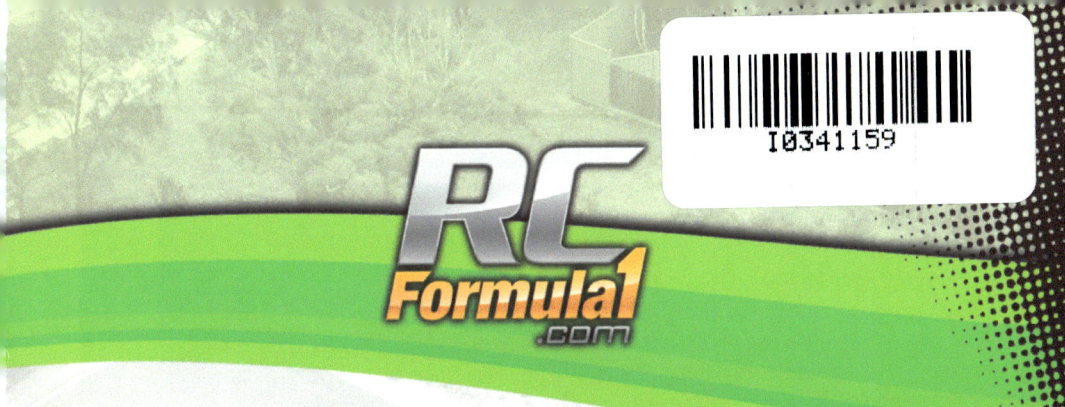

Essential Touring Car RC Racer's Guide

Dave B Stevens

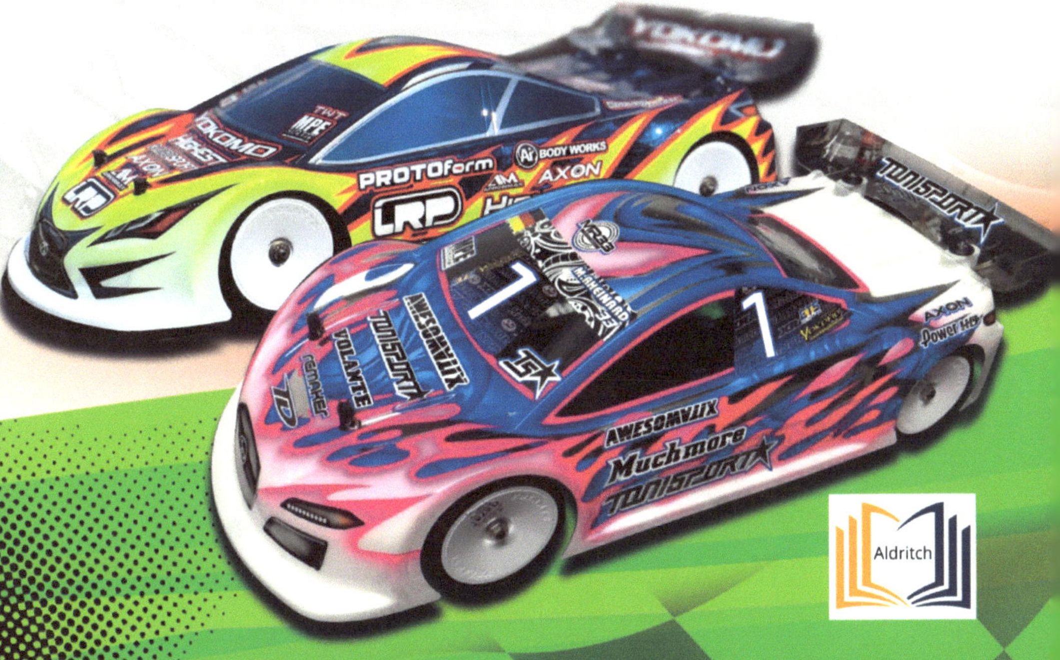

Aldritch

Copyright © 2020 David Bryan Stevens. **www.DaveBStevens.com**

Speed Secrets © 2016-2020 Ryan Maker. **rcmaker.com.au**

History chapter © 2014-2020 Craig Howard. **theRCracer.com**

All rights reserved. No part of this publication may be reproduced, stored in a retrieval system, or transmitted in any form or by any means, electronic, mechanical, photocopying, recording or otherwise, without the prior permission of the copyright holder.

Published by Dave B Stevens, Aldritch Publishing, Melbourne, Australia.

ISBN 978-0-6485811-2-3: First printed in 2020. Reprinted and print on demand 2021.

Graphic Design: Evie Diakogeorgaki.
Illustrations: Ruwan Prasanga.
Technical Contribution: Ryan Maker, Marc Rheinard, Ronald Völker, Alexander Hagberg, Jan Ratheisky, David Spashett, Andy Cooke.
Additional Case Studies: Valentin Hettrich, Olivier Bultynck, Alexandre Duchet, Simon Lauter, Max Mächler.
Additional Contribution: Aaron Stevens.

Photo Credits: Thank you to the following for their kind permission to reproduce their photos in this book. The page numbers for each of their photos are listed after the contributor's name (t=top; m=middle; b=bottom; l=left; r=right):

Evan Black: 31; Randy Caster (1upracing.com): 67; Dave Calwell: 229; J Cascella: 211 2nd photo from bottom; Courtney: 113, 118; Steeve Daver: 61b, 86t; Euro Touring Series (eurorcseries.com & rc-car-pics.de): 37, 47, 90b, 93bl, 93br, 106, 162bl, 162br, 190, 191, 192, 194, 196, 198, 199, 200, 201, 204, 240, 255, 259; Alexander Hagberg: 231; Craig Howard: 228; John Karnaros: 214t; George Lakovou: 217; Eric Lamme: 222; Werner Lane: 215t, 218; Ryan Maker (rcmaker.com.au): 45, 49, 53, 54, 56, 58, 60, 64b, 65, 66, 68tl, 70bl, 71, 73, 74b, 76, 77t, 77bl, 79, 82r, 83, 84t, 84bl, 86b, 87, 128, 132t, 136b, 159tl, 159tr, 170; Andy Moore: 225; Justin Pugh: 211b; Racer Magazine: 220t; Ben Rayment: 220b; Marc Rheinard (@Marc-Rheinard-RC): cover photo of his car and self, 12, 17, 64t, 215b, 223, 224, 226, 227; Toni Rheinard (www.tonisport.de): 61t, 68tr, 70br, 77br, 84br, 119l, 158t, 159b, 171, 189, 247, 248; Greg Rojna: 211 2nd photo from top; Nick Sanfilippo: title page track, rear cover track; Nicola Sbrana (www.nicola670paint.com): 43, 51, 63, 68b, 78, 81, 85l, 90t, 108, 156, 162t, 212b, 213b; Michael Sherman (www.speedyrc.com.au): 151; Omar Siddig: 219; Aaron Stevens: 11, 14, 19, 21, 22, 24, 25, 28, 30, 32, 44, 69, 80b, 88, 125t, 131, 138, 140, 163, 172, 210m, 201b, 211t, 213m, 214m; Matt Subotsch: 36; Andreas Teubl (@A83 Speedgraphix): 35, 80t, 85r, 93t, 112, 205, 206, 207, 208, 209, 212t, 212m; Kévin Thomassin (@KevinThomassinPhotographies): 39, 40, 55, 57, 59, 100, 102, 114, 125b, 137, 174, 175, 178, 180, 183, 184, 185, 186, 188, 253; Ronald Völker (@RonaldVoelkerRC): cover photo of his car, and self, 13, 18, 230.

All other photography is by the author.

Table of Contents

chapter 1

Introduction — 11

Foreword — Marc Rheinard — 12
Foreword – Ronald Völker — 13
Author's Preface — 14
Introduction — 15
How To Use This Book — 15
The Cars — 17

chapter 2

The Process of Driving Faster — 19

Introduction — 20
Setup Theory — 20
Setup Sheets — 22
Weight Transfer – the Holy Grail — 23
The Racing Line — 24
   Braking Point — 25
   Turn-in Point — 25
   Apex — 26
      Wide Corners — 26
      Geometric Apex — 27
      Late Apex — 28
      Early Apex — 28
      Overtaking on a Corner — 29
      The Karting Apex — 29
      Chicanes — 30
      Hairpins — 31
      Sweepers — 31
   Slipstream Overtaking — 32
   The Position of the Next Corner — 33
   Increasing Corner Speed — 33
Mapping the Track — 35
   Modified Racing Line — 37
Conquering a New Track — 38

Table of Contents

Perfect Practice Makes Perfect 40
Driver Etiquette and Traffic 41
   Lapping 41
   Staggered Start Passing 41
   How to Pass 41
   Resolving Disputes 42
   After a Crash 42
   Hitting Someone From Behind 43
   Marshals 43

chapter 3

The Build 44

Introduction 45
The Rules 47
The Build 48
   Preparation 48
   Chassis Assembly 50
   Suspension Components 51
   Lower Bulkheads and Chassis 52
   Drivetrain 52
   Upper Bulkheads and Chassis Finishing 55
   Shock Absorbers 56
   Roll Bars 58
   Steering Rack 60
   Servo 60
   Finishing Touches 62
   Elements 63
   Electronics 64

chapter 4

Initial Setup 69

Introduction 70
Droop 70
Roll Bars 71
Servo and Steering Alignment 73

Table of Contents

Ride Height _____ 75
Camber _____ 77
Tweak _____ 78
Finishing Touches _____ 79

chapter 5

Body Shell Mounting _____ 80
Introduction _____ 81
Body Position _____ 82
Body Height _____ 83
Wheel Arches _____ 84
Painting _____ 85
Bumper Foam _____ 86
Wing _____ 87

chapter 6

Car Setup Reference _____ 88
Ackermann _____ 91
Anti-dive (front) _____ 93
Anti-squat/Pro-squat (Rear) _____ 94
Arm Sweep _____ 95
Battery Position _____ 96
Belt Tension _____ 96
Bodies _____ 97
Bump Steer _____ 97
Camber _____ 98
Camber Gain _____ 101
Chassis Stiffness (Flex) _____ 103
Caster _____ 104
Centre of Gravity _____ 105
Damping _____ 105
   Length of Shock _____ 106
   Oil _____ 107
   Piston Holes _____ 108
   Position _____ 109

Table of Contents

   Preload 110
   Rebound 111
   Springs 113
Differential 115
   Gear Diff 115
   Ball Diff 116
   Diff Height 118
Droop 119
   Rear Droop 122
   Front Droop 123
ESC Settings 124
Flex 125
Gearing & Rollout 126
   Gearing for Final Drive Ratio or Rollout? 126
   Final Drive Ratios 126
   Gear Ratio Charts 127
   So What FDR Should You Start With? 127
   What Rollout Should You Start With? 128
   Gear Mesh 128
   End Bell Timing 128
   Tuning Gearing for the Lowest Lap Times 129
   Motor Temperature 129
Kick-up/Anti-dive (Front) 130
Motor Mount Location 132
Pro-squat 133
Radio Settings 133
Ride Height 134
   Overview 134
   Ride Height Split 134
   Starting Ride Height 135
   Measuring Ride Height 135
   Left vs Right Side Ride Height 137
   Changing the Ride Height 137
   Ride Height Interactions 138
   Ride Height and Tyres 138
Roll Bars 139
Roll Centre 141
Rollout 143
Shock Absorber 143
Solid Axle (Spool) 143
Steering Arm Ball-cup Location 144
Steering Linkage Angle 144

Table of Contents

Steering Throw/Lock _____ 144
Toe _____ 145
Track Width _____ 149
Tyres & Additives _____ 151
   Rubber Tyres _____ *152*
   Foam Tyres _____ *152*
   Tyre Preparation _____ *153*
   Additive _____ *153*
   Tyre Warmers _____ *155*
   Wheel Balancing _____ *156*
Weight _____ 157
   Centre of Gravity _____ *157*
   Weight Balance (Side-to-Side) _____ *157*
   Moving Weight (Front-to-Rear) _____ *160*
   Adding Weight to Increase Steering or Rear Traction _____ *160*
Wheelbase _____ 161
Wings _____ 162

chapter 7

Tweak _____ 163

What is Tweak? _____ 164
Tweak Checklist _____ 164
Testing for Chassis Twist _____ 166
Correcting Suspension Tweak _____ 168

chapter 8

Case Studies _____ 172

Carpet Case Studies _____ 173
   Modified _____ *175*
   Stock _____ *185*
Asphalt Case Studies _____ 189
   Modified _____ *191*
   Stock _____ *199*

Table of Contents

chapter 9

Other Body Shells — 205
Touring Cars — 206
Vintage Trans Am — 210
GT — 212
V8 Supercars — 214

chapter 10

History — 215

appendix A

eBook — 233

appendix B

Glossary — 234

appendix C

Beginner's Guide — 238
Buying Considerations — 238
A Beginner's Story — 239
Common Build Errors — 240
Tyre Gluing — 246
Setup Diary — 246
Tools — 247
Lipo Battery Safety — 248

Table of Contents

appendix D

Checklists — 249

Maintenance — 250
- *After Run Checks* — 250
- *Between Events* — 251
- *Re-building a Car* — 252

Correcting Key Balance Issues — 254
- *Traction – How to Increase* — 254
- *Steering* — 256
  - Too Much Steering (Oversteer) — 256
  - Not Enough Steering (Understeer) — 258
  - Steering Response Changes for No Apparent Reason — 259
- *Traction Rolling* — 260
- *Easier to Drive – How To* — 261

Troubleshooting — 262
- *Car Wanders on the Straight* — 262
- *Change of Direction (Chicane)* — 262
- *Fast Sweeper Cornering* — 262
- *Car 'Hops' or 'Chatters' Across the Track* — 262
- *Tyres Picking Up Carpet Debris from Track* — 262
- *Inconsistent Handling* — 263
- *Lacking Acceleration or Started Oversteering* — 263

Quick Reference — 265

Chapter 1

Introduction

Foreword — Marc Rheinard

From 1994, my father had a big hobby shop with an indoor and outdoor asphalt track. So after school I always went there to drive RC, and I really liked it!

After winning my first World Championship title in 2004, I signed a contract with Tamiya including all travel costs and a monthly salary. To be a full-time professional racer was my dream come true and all up I enjoyed driving for Tamiya for about 22 years.

This book has a massive amount of information and many tips and tricks useful for everyone trackside. Nobody knows everything, so it's always good to have the opportunity to open the book and find the information you need, whether you're a beginner or a pro.

The key for any driver to improve is track time. The more you are on the track, the more you improve your driving, learn how the car works and how to set it up. It's also good if you practice with a teammate or friend to learn to drive in a battle on the track. There is a big difference between qualifying and finals. Many people are good in qualifying, but in the finals they are not used to fighting with another driver and therefore make mistakes.

Making a mistake is always frustrating, but never give up during a run. This is the most important thing for a racer. There is always the chance that other drivers may make mistakes and you can still get a decent result. Never give up!

Marc Rheinard

- ✓ 3 x Touring Car IFMAR World Champion
- ✓ 2 x 1/12th IFMAR World Champion
- ✓ 3 x European Touring Car Champion
- ✓ 8 x National Touring Car Champion
- ✓ 7 x Reedy Race USA TC Champion

Author's note:

Marc Rheinard is one of the world's most talented drivers. Few achieve the title of World Champion, fewer still repeat this feat. Marc has not only accomplished this in Touring Cars, but also in 1/12th Scale. Marc created the MR33 brand of racing parts and accessories and has allowed me to use these as examples throughout this book. He was not paid for his support.

Foreword — Ronald Völker

After many years with Yokomo, I am excited to take on a new challenge with Mugen Seiki as my main sponsor. I also have a great long term relationship with LRP, which will continue.

I am using my experience to assist Mugen Seiki to become strong in electric on-road. They are a small, highly motivated company with an excellent reputation in nitro on-road/off-road cars. The materials quality in their new MTC2 Touring Car is the best I've ever seen, and I have no doubt this is going to be very successful.

My focus is to help customers and teammates so we have a large number of happy people running a Mugen branded Touring Car.

When I'm helping other drivers, sometimes their cars are well balanced, but often they have issues with basic setup or tweak. This book can assist with those problems. The most important thing is to have fun, and that's harder to do with a misbehaving car.

Whether you see RC car racing as a hobby or a sport, there are endless things to learn. This book is an excellent source of information, and you can check it whenever you need answers or are looking for ideas.

Ronald Völker

- ✓ Touring Car IFMAR World Champion
- ✓ 9 x European Champion
- ✓ 15 x National Champion
- ✓ 5 x Euro Touring Series Overall Champion
- ✓ 3 x Reedy Race USA TC Champion

Author's note:

Ronald Völker started driving at the age of four and has been a full-time professional driver since 2009. One of the best performers in the sport, he is consistently on the top step at major races around the world. He was not paid to support this book.

Author's Preface

In 2007, my 11-year-old son, Aaron, bought an RC Touring Car on eBay. As soon as I saw it I had to have one for myself, and Aaron and I spent most weekends at the track from then on.

There is a lot of information on the web about setting up RC Touring Cars. However, it is often hard to find, incomplete, brand-specific, out of date or on a forum where the discussion lacks the context to make it truly useful.

I wrote this book to create a comprehensive manual that racers can follow to improve their lap times, regardless of their skill level or the car they drive. I spent 30 years as a business consultant, and part of my skill set is to extract technical experience from experts in the field, pull in relevant information from multiple sources, and present it in an easy to apply "how-to" format.

About the Author

In 2019 Dave wrote *Essential 1/12th and F1 RC Racer's Guide* which sold in 27 countries.

In 2013 he set a Guinness World Record for: The longest distance covered by a battery-operated remote-controlled car. A record he held for three years.

In 2012 Dave launched www.RCformula1.com. In the early years, it was the only dedicated RC F1 website, and it is still the most read, with nearly 7 million page views as of late 2020.

Dave has written for a number of magazines, including his regular column in Racing Lines. He is a former president of the Templestowe Flat Track Racers RC club and a former board member of the Victorian On Road Tracks Executive Committee.

He also writes fantasy fiction and lives in Melbourne, Australia with his wife and sons.

Connect with Dave via: Facebook facebook.com/DaveBStevens.Author
                       Web   www.DaveBStevens.com

Introduction

This book provides in-depth information on Touring Cars. Specifically, 1/10 scale on-road electric 4WD Touring Cars (often referred to as ISTC when using saloon/sedan bodies).

Touring Cars are fantastic for beginners as they are relatively easy to drive.

It is very achievable to have a car which has sufficient rear-end grip and still has enough steering to turn tight corners, under almost all track conditions. This guide provides you with the information to set up your car to be easy, and fun, to drive fast.

Every weekend, you will find Touring Cars racing around club tracks throughout the world. Some drivers are racing with their friends to have fun, others are trying to win at club level or a local competition. Most countries have regional racing, nationally organised competitions, and of course, there are world championships.

The Modified Touring Car class has been an International Federation of Model Auto Racing (IFMAR) World Championship class since 1998. In the last few years, the Spec Touring Car class (13.5 motor with Non-Timing ESC) was added as an official IFMAR class. A fantastic range of Touring Car classes are raced at local clubs including VTA, GT, and others. A range of motors are also available from the sedate 25.5 turn to the super quick Modified/open motors like the 4.5 turn. No matter your level of skill, and how fast you want to go, Touring Cars have a class to suit!

Whether you are an experienced racer looking for an edge over your competition, or a complete beginner, this book was designed to provide the answers you're looking for. It provides a complete, step-by-step reference to these fantastic cars.

How To Use This Book

Appendix B – Glossary on page *215* defines core technical terms referred to in this book.

The Process of Driving Faster starting on page *19* covers setup theory, a driving tutorial, and how to apply this theory to any track.

If you are a beginner, then your next step is to check out *Appendix C – Beginner's Guide* on page *238*.

The Build on page *44* takes you step-by-step through building your car perfectly.

Initial Setup on page *69* covers how to nail the initial setup.

Body Shell Mounting on page *80* provides tips for obtaining the greatest advantage from your body shell.

You should now be ready to hit the track with a car that is fast from the first lap.

Car Setup Reference starting on page *88*, covers the A–Z of setup settings from Ackermann to Wings and everything in between. I've also labelled each setting option as Basic, Intermediate or Advanced.

Tweak starting on page *163* covers how to ensure all your tyres touch the ground with equal pressure and what happens if they don't. It also describes how to fix a car that is "tweaked".

Case Studies starting on page *172* describes actual race meetings, and how skilled drivers approached their setup, what changes they made, why, and the results.

Appendix D – Checklists on page *249* covers all the common problems and situations you might encounter. Car is spinning out? Wanders on the straight? Doesn't have enough steering? We've got you covered.

Other Body Shells on page *205* might provide you with inspiration for painting scale replica bodies for display or for classes such as VTA and GT.

This book is available in eBook format for ease of reference at the track. The eBook is available at a discount for those who have purchased the physical book. For details refer to page *215*.

The Cars

This book covers 1/10 scale on-road electric 4WD Touring Cars with 2S lipo batteries.

Marc Rheinard's Awesomatix A800MMX

Ronald Völker's Mugen MTC2

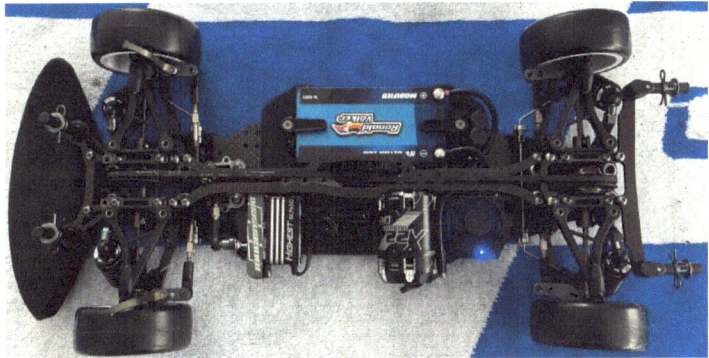

Chapter 2
The Process of Driving Faster

Introduction

Being able to drive faster, on a given track, is a process which involves the following steps:

1. Determine a base setup for the track.
2. Map the Racing Line for the track.
3. Practice the Racing Line for the track.
4. Tune your car's setup so you can drive it as quickly as you are able, as close to the Racing Line as possible.
5. Practice the Racing Line for the track until qualifying starts.

Setup Theory

A car's handling is determined by the contact patch of the tyre on the racing surface. In a full-size production car, that area is about the same as a size 10 shoe. In an RC car, it might be the size of your fingernail or smaller.

How the tyres interact with the track determines how the car corners, accelerates and brakes. So tyre choice is the most important factor in car handling. However, at most large race meetings, a control tyre is used, meaning everyone has the same brand and compound of tyre. So the advantage goes to those who set up their car so that those tyres provide the right amount of grip at the right time.

Ignoring other factors for the moment, the easier the car is to drive, the faster you will be able to drive it. Changing the car's setup will make the car easier to drive near its performance limit. This should allow you to drive it faster.

In this book, we explain what each setting is, why it changes the behaviour of the car, how to make each change and the result you should expect.

Make small changes, one at a time and measure the result based on what you were trying to achieve (refer to Mapping the Track on page 35). Note whether the car felt better or worse and any impact on lap times. We say small changes because adding a 0.5mm shim or changing a setting by 0.5 degree may make a noticeable difference, and if you jump to a 2mm shim or 1.5 degree change, then you may miss the sweet spot.

We recommend that you keep track of your setup changes and record which setups work best at different tracks under various conditions.

A car that "feels" faster is not necessarily turning faster lap times. Use a stopwatch or timing system to check if it really is quicker, and not just easier to drive.

For the car to respond correctly to setup changes, it must be in good working order. In other words: the car is not tweaked (page 163), the suspension is free, dampers (page 105) and differential (page 115) are correctly built, no broken binding or loose parts, and the car has proper weight balance left-to-right (page 157).

Many setup adjustments interact with other settings. For example, changing the ride height will also change the droop. These interactions are explained under the relevant headings.

Fine-tuning the setup will make the car easier to drive near its performance limit. This should allow you to drive it faster.

Start with a base setup, make changes so that the car drives the lines you want (see The Racing Line on page 24), then stiffen the car up as much as practical while making sure it is still as easy for you to drive as possible. As you gain experience, you will be able to short cut this process.

Use our After Race Checklist on page 250 to identify problems before the next run.

Setup Sheets

Team Driver Setup Sheets can be a useful reference, and it is helpful to see what changes professional drivers have made. However, copying another driver's setup sheet without understanding why each change was made can cause a car to be undriveable: the track conditions are probably different, they may not have recorded their setup completely accurately, their driving preferences and skill level are almost certainly different to yours. Note: setup sheets are normally based on finals, once the best setup has been determined.

Different cars have unique handling characteristics. Even with the same chassis, driver style varies. That is why it is not recommended that you copy a world champion's car setup without understanding the settings. Instead, identify the differences between their setup and your car's setup and make one change at a time. Determine whether your car handling is better or worse, based on your skill level and driving style, and fine tune from there.

It is better to make small incremental changes. Most chassis will have one basic setup for carpet and another for asphalt, and this is usually a better place to start than how a pro driver sets up their car. These setup sheets may be found in your car's manual or be available on the manufacturer's website. If your manufacturer only has a carpet setup, then refer to Asphalt Case Studies on page 189 for guidance on the difference between carpet and asphalt setups and how others have approached this issue.

Don't hesitate to ask for setup tips from the local fast drivers. Treat their advice like a pro driver's setup sheet by making one change they suggest at a time and noting the result. By doing this, you are refining your own setup knowledge.

Weight Transfer — the Holy Grail

Weight transfer refers to the redistribution of weight supported by each tyre during acceleration, braking and cornering. Understanding weight transfer is the key to understanding car setup and handling.

When a car is at rest, it has a certain amount of weight on each tyre. By transferring weight from one tyre to another (front-to-rear or side-to-side), the loaded tyre will be pushed harder onto the racing surface and, therefore, will have more grip. Equally, the inside tyre on a corner will have less grip.

This book explains all the setup settings available to you, how changing these will allow the transfer of more weight, or less weight, during racing and how this affects the handling of your car.

Car setup is a matter of compromise. For example, transferring more weight to the front tyres will provide more initial steering, but reduces rear traction. The aim is to set up your car so it is easy for you to drive quickly and consistently from lap to lap while providing sufficient rear traction and sufficient steering. Of course, your definition of driving quickly will depend on your experience and skill as a driver. Regardless of how well you drive, it is possible for you to set up your car so you can drive it as quickly and consistently as your current ability allows.

Good setup is all about controlling weight transfer.

The Racing Line

The racing line is the fastest path through any corner and identifying it is an essential skill for any driver wanting to lower their lap times.

Driving the fastest laps possible is a combination of two competing goals:

1. driving the shortest possible distance around the track, and
2. keeping the car's cornering speed as high as possible by minimising the angle of the corners.

By using all the space available on the track, your car can travel in a straighter line and therefore drive through the corner at a faster speed (keeping in mind *Wide Corners* on page *26*).

You should experiment with different lines, watch the fast guys and talk to other drivers at the track. On some tracks, the most common racing line will show up as a darker, or even black, area on the track.

Ignoring traffic for the moment, the racing line is determined by the following factors:

- Braking point.
- Turn-in point.
- Apex.
- The position and direction of the next corner.
- The acceleration a car has available (a Modified car's racing line may differ from a Stock car's racing line).

We will now break down each of these factors:

Braking Point

The aim when braking before a corner is to slow down just enough to clip the apex (defined on the next page). If you enter the corner too fast, you will miss the apex (understeer). If you enter the corner too slowly, you may need to accelerate mid-turn. Both scenarios mean you won't be going as quickly as you could be.

It makes sense to brake earlier when learning the track and getting familiar with your car, then gradually reduce the braking distance as your confidence and experience grows. Ideally, you should be off the brakes before turning into the corner. For pro drivers, a slight brake pressure on entry can help to reduce understeer and provide a better turn-in (known as trail braking).

Other factors include:

- Modified motors have greater braking power than Stock class motors.
- Braking too early may result in a slow lap.
- Braking too late may result in overshooting the corner and a slow lap (or in the worst-case scenario, a broken car).

For each corner, choose a braking marker. This is a specific point on the track (or to one side of it) that doesn't move, which you can use as a consistent reference for precisely where to brake.

Turn-in Point

To get the racing line right, it is vital to turn-in at the correct point. Leave it too late and you'll understeer, missing the apex. Turn-in too soon and you'll clip the apex/curb, upset the car and have to adjust your line mid-corner, losing speed.

Pick a spot on the track as your turn-in point and note it on your track map (refer to *Mapping the Track* on page 35). Adjust this turn-in point during practice until you're happy with your line through the corner.

Apex

The apex is the point at which you are closest to the inside of the corner (also known as the clipping point). Once you have hit the apex, you should be able to reduce your steering input and increase the throttle as the car exits the corner.

In general terms, there are three different types of apex. These are summarised in the table below, and you would normally select the best apex for a corner depending on traffic and the position of the next corner:

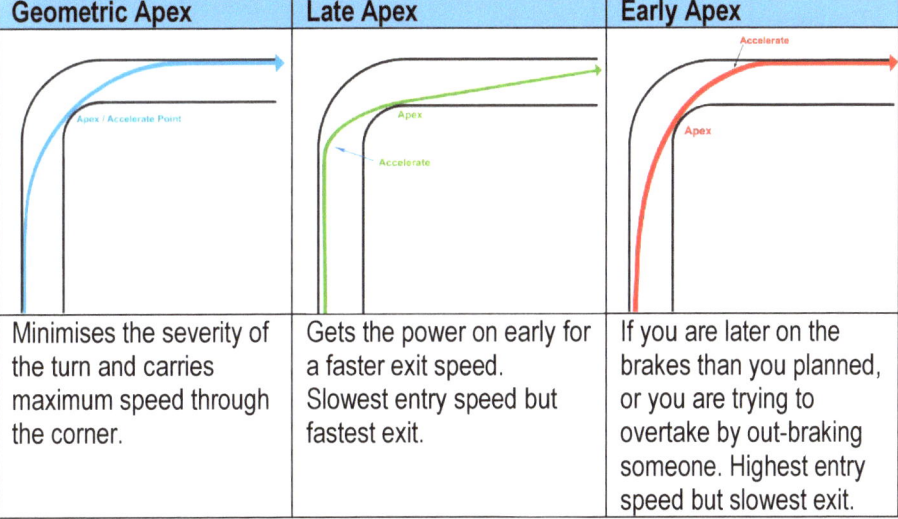

Geometric Apex	Late Apex	Early Apex
Minimises the severity of the turn and carries maximum speed through the corner.	Gets the power on early for a faster exit speed. Slowest entry speed but fastest exit.	If you are later on the brakes than you planned, or you are trying to overtake by out-braking someone. Highest entry speed but slowest exit.

As previously stated, by using all the space available on the track, your car can travel in a straighter line and therefore drive through the corner at a faster speed.

Each of the above is discussed in more detail on the following pages.

Wide Corners

In real racing, using the full width of the racetrack is normally faster, but in RC this is not necessarily the case. Refer to the optimal line around the example track on page 36.

If the entry or exit of a corner is very wide (the track width is wider than required for the racing line) then touching the outside of the track on the way in and the outside of the track on the way out increases the distance travelled and slows the overall lap time. In this situation, some trial and error may be required to determine the optimum time to turn in.

Any part of the track that is not on the racing line is often dirty, with reduced grip, and should be avoided.

Geometric Apex

The geometric apex of a constant radius corner is the central point on the inside of the corner.

Hitting the geometric apex is good for carrying speed and minimising turn severity.

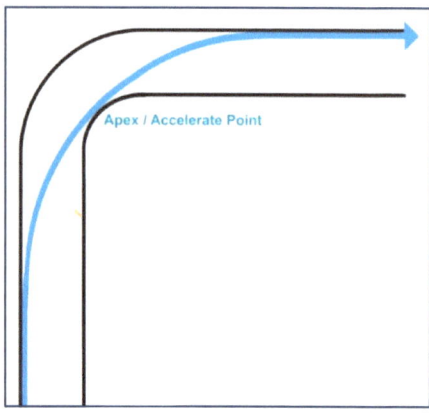

The fastest way through a 90-degree corner is to touch the outside of the track on the approach, hit the geometric apex of the corner, and then swing out in an even curve to meet the outside edge of the track. By following a symmetrical, curved line you will take the corner as fast as possible by minimising the tightness of the corner. This minimises cornering force, freeing up grip for maintaining speed.

The geometric apex is exactly halfway around this corner.

Advantages:

- Smooths out the corner efficiently.
- Maintains momentum (particularly useful for Stock/lower powered cars).
- Reduces the chances of understeer or oversteer (especially helpful in low grip conditions).
- Preserves tyre life.

Disadvantages:

While it is the fastest way to drive the current corner, it is not necessarily the fastest way to drive the next part of the track and therefore may not produce the fastest lap times in all situations.

Late Apex

If a straight follows the corner, then the ideal racing line for maximum speed over the corner, plus the straight, is a late apex. Although the car is slower into the corner when compared to a geometric apex, it positions the car to accelerate much earlier. Overall, the time over that part of the track, from the corner entry to the end of the straight, is quicker.

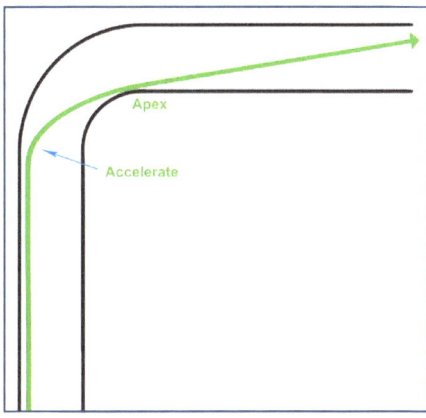

Accelerating early as the car passes the clipping point means it will be faster down the following straight. The driver who accelerates sooner and/or harder has a large advantage, and a late apex may help maximise that advantage.

Advantages:

- Increases the chances of a fast lap in a powerful car (Modified).
- Allows the power to be applied earlier.
- Maximises the use of any straights following the corner.

Disadvantages:

- Requires earlier braking.
- May not be the fastest path in a lower powered car.

In the right circumstances, Ronald Völker often takes a late apex. He will brake early and smoothly, gaining the early acceleration advantage from apex to exit.

Early Apex

An Early Apex can be faster for an understeering car.

We can also use it for overtaking as described below.

Overtaking on a Corner

We've seen that the fastest way around a track is to follow the racing line. If you are closely following a car that is following this racing line, then they may approach the corner from the outside of the track. This provides an opportunity to brake late and take an early apex, darting up the inside of your opponent (the red racing line on the diagram below right). Although you will probably run wide to maintain your corner speed, you should have nosed in front of the other car. You may also have disrupted their concentration and/or forced them off the line that they wanted to take. Pass accomplished.

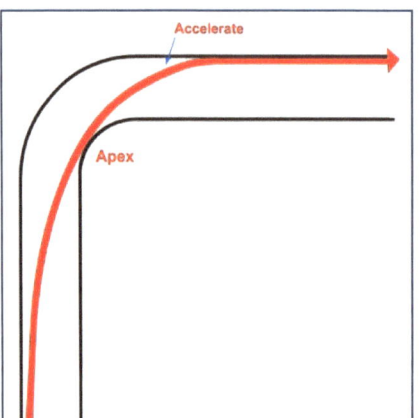
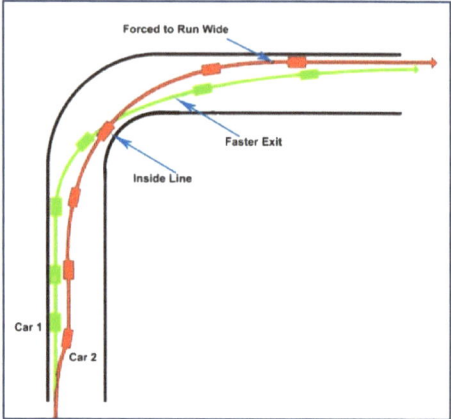

To defend against the above, you need to take a late apex while slowing sufficiently not to hit the car passing you, and then accelerate early and shoot back past them while they are running wide.

Of course, once you have another car close on your tail, you leave yourself open to the above passing scenario if you stick to the racing line. You may, therefore, wish to drive closer to the inside of the track to prevent the above overtaking move. Your choice to not drive the racing line will slow your lap times, but by not leaving a gap, you should retain the position.

The Karting Apex

The best racing line for a low-powered car (such as a 25.5 motor) can be the Karting Line (in some circumstances). This is a wider line that doesn't hit the apex. Karts don't have good brakes or quick

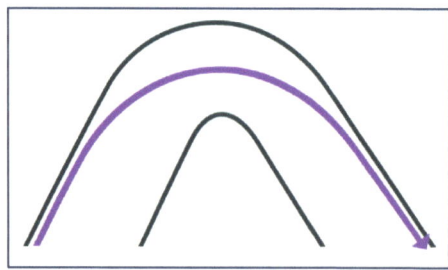

acceleration and therefore focus on maintaining momentum around the track.

Faster cars can also use the Karting Line when traction is low, as it maintains as much momentum as possible without relying heavily on acceleration.

Driving Tips

- Only brake in a straight line and don't jam the brakes on. Reduce the radio's brake End Point Adjustment, if necessary, until you get used to smooth braking.
- Accelerate smoothly out of corners so you don't lose the back end.
- Experiment to find the best line around each corner for your driving style.
- If you can't turn as tightly as you would like, slow down. Otherwise, overshooting a corner will more than lose any gain from entering the corner faster. Then adjust your setup for the next run so you have sufficient steering to take the corner the way you want to.

Chicanes

A chicane is a shallow corner in one direction, followed by a shallow corner in the other direction. Depending on the corners preceding and following the chicane, it can often be driven at high speed. This requires a car which will change direction quickly (refer to page 262) and examination of the chicane for the straightest possible line through it (refer to the examples on page 36). Chicanes can be a difficult part of the track to drive quickly due to the fast steering inputs required without upsetting the car.

Hairpins

A hairpin is a corner which changes the direction of the car by 180 degrees. The fastest line around a hairpin is a very late apex (about three-quarters of the way around the bend). A guide point is that halfway through the turn, you should be roughly in the middle of the track.

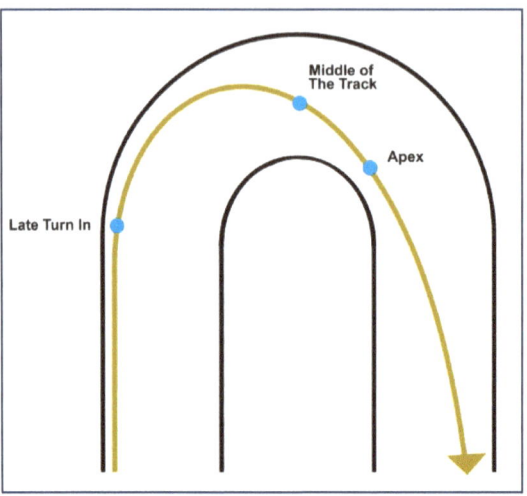

Sweepers

A sweeper is a long corner. Because the corner is not very sharp, the steering input is less, and because of this, the corner may be taken much faster than a sharper corner.

With some sweepers, it is faster to follow the corner as closely as possible, while with others, running wide may lead to a faster exit. Unfortunately, it is not practical to provide diagrams for every scenario.

Livery of the famous Mazda 787B — winner of the 1991 Le Mans 24 HR

The Process of Driving Faster 2

Sweepers are often at the start or end of the straight.

If the sweeper is entered relatively slowly, because of the prior corner, then you are often accelerating during most of the sweeper and may hug the inside throughout and still be at full speed as early as possible on the straight — example on the left below.

If the sweeper is entered at high speed, then it may be easier to think of the sweeper as two separate corners — example on the right below.

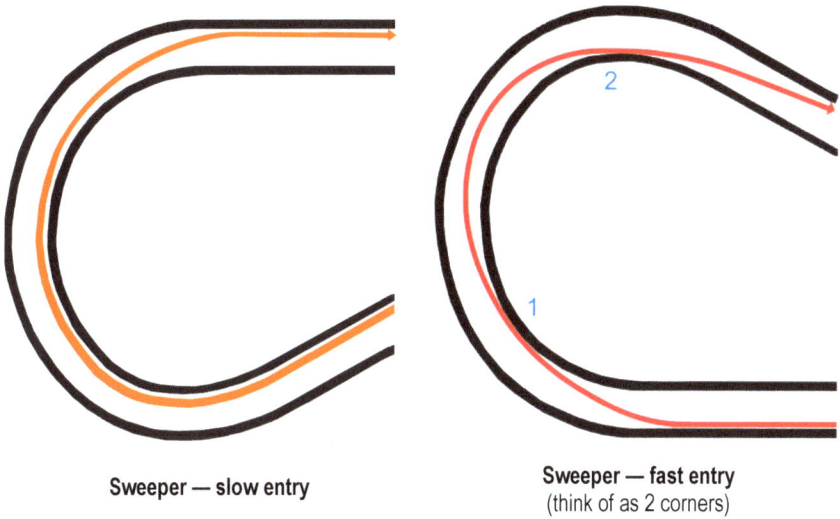

Sweeper — slow entry

Sweeper — fast entry
(think of as 2 corners)

Diagrams are examples only and will not apply to every sweeper.

Slipstream Overtaking

In RC racing, using the slipstream of the car in front is not commonly practised at club level. It is very difficult to get right, and the straights are not usually long enough for it to make a significant difference. There are exceptions but in general, tucking your car closely in behind the car in front is difficult and risky to both cars in RC.

The Position of the Next Corner

The fastest way through a 90-degree corner is discussed above under the heading Geometric Apex. However, we aren't just trying to take one corner as fast as possible, we're trying to drive a complete lap as fast as possible, and the position and direction of the next corner affect the racing line of the current corner. For example, if the next corner is a left-hander you'll need to move over to the right-hand side of the track (orange line below), and therefore will need to apex later and take a tighter, slower line. However, if the next corner is another right-hander, a wider faster line can be used (red line below):

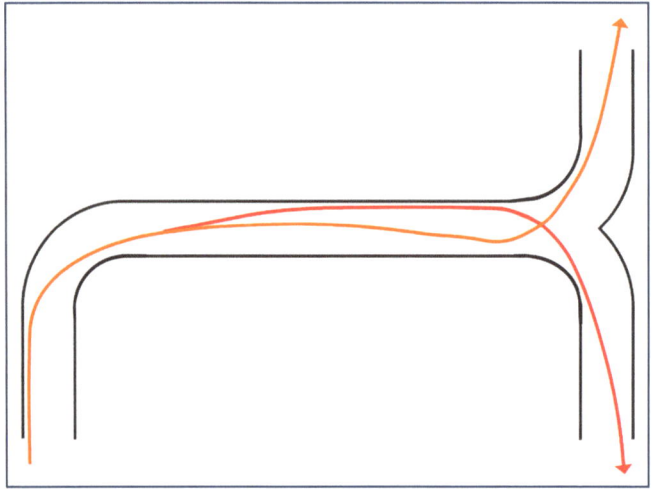

When there are a series of corners, it is better to view them as one large corner and focus on maximising your exit speed from the last corner. The early apex technique maintains car stability so you can navigate these multiple corners. The last corner is then taken with a late apex for maximum acceleration.

Increasing Corner Speed

Now that we know how to find the best line through a corner, the next step is to drive it as quickly as possible.

"Slow in, fast out" is the strategy of slowing more on the approach to the corner to ensure that you hit your apex and get back on the throttle as soon as possible. It is a useful mantra to keep in mind when first learning about cornering. However, we don't want to enter the corner slowly. We only want to slow the car the minimum amount so we can hit the chosen apex.

The fastest lap means always driving your car on the absolute limit of the available grip. When you brake, leave the braking as late as possible so you can use all the available grip to brake the car down to the speed you wish to take the corner (which is ideally the fastest speed that your car can take the corner). When you stop braking, this makes grip available for turning (which is why hard braking and turning at the same time can make you lose control, as well as scrubbing off speed). As you pass the apex, reduce the steering input to make grip available for acceleration.

Pro drivers often reduce the Steering Throw (page 144) to maximise corner speed. You can see examples of this in the Case Studies chapter on page 172.

Sections of a Corner

Ideally, braking should be smooth and fluid. Steering should also be smooth and fluid. Sudden or jerky braking/steering can upset the balance of the car, causing it to oversteer or understeer.

Tapping the brakes transfers weight forward for cornering which gives the car more grip available for steering.

The perfect corner involves tightening the steering until the apex and then gradually reducing the steering as you accelerate. If you find yourself increasing or correcting the steering during the corner, after the initial turn-in, you've probably taken the wrong line.

The greatest demand on the tyres' grip occurs between the turn-in point and the apex. It is important not to accelerate or brake during this part of the turn; you want to maintain a constant speed.

When accelerating, you will not be able to use all the power of a Modified car until you're completely in a straight line. However, if you're in a less powerful car, you can apply the throttle much closer to the apex.

Smooth braking and steering are factors that separate the professional driver from the club racer.

Mapping the Track

Now that you know how to determine the racing line for any corner (refer to page 24) you should sketch out the racing line for the entire track. This is your map of the track. Then practice driving it. Once you are comfortable that you are driving the racing line as close as possible, it may become obvious that the car is not following the racing line in certain sections as closely as you wish. By changing the setup of the car, you can make it easier to drive the racing line. For example, the car may not follow the sweeper the way you'd like, or it may take hairpins too wide. These issues may be corrected by changing the car setup to allow you to drive the racing line you have selected more closely and therefore reduce your lap times.

Refer to *Appendix D – Checklists* on page 249 for how to correct various issues with car handling.

Walking the track can be a useful way of determining the racing line. This technique is particularly useful in chicanes to determine the straightest path through. When walking the track don't walk on the racing line itself as you may track dirt or dust from your shoes over it, changing the grip level.

On most tracks, your car will spend more time in the low-speed corners than in high-speed corners or on the straight. Therefore, that is where your biggest time gains might be made. For that reason, you may wish to adjust your gearing (refer to page 126) to increase acceleration out of corners, at the expense of top speed on the straight.

The Process of Driving Faster

Putting It All Together

The following racing line (in green) is a good starting point and can be adjusted to suit your skill level and driving style. It is suited to lower powered cars (for Modified cars refer to the next page).

The example track is quite wide in places, and it would be much slower to use the full track width when cornering (as discussed under *Wide Corners* on page *26*).

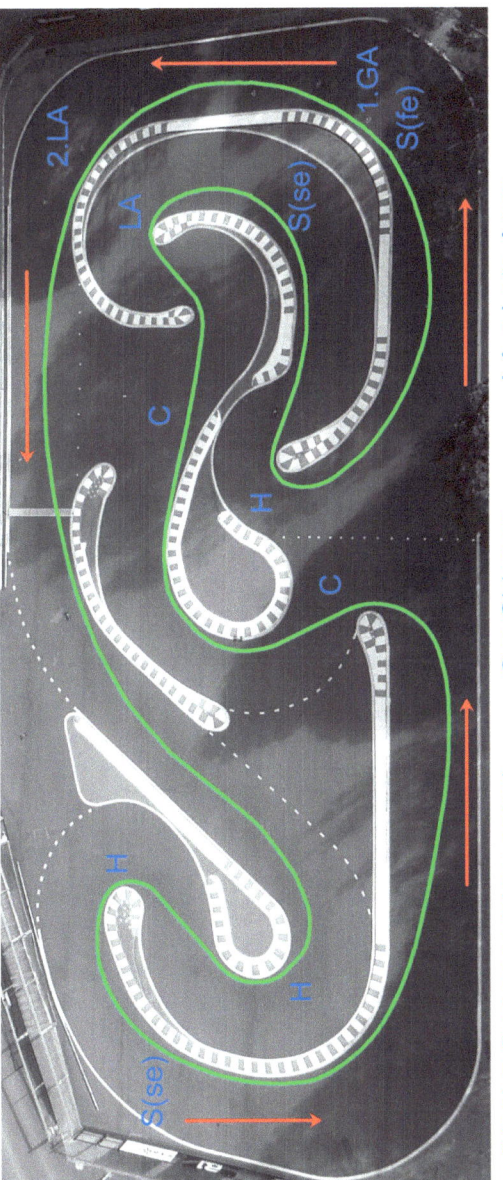

Modified Racing Line

The sheer power available to Modified cars encourages a different racing line. Although similar to the above, it is more point to point, with less arc and hugging the inside white line wherever possible. Squeeze on throttle, full power in a straight line, full brakes, turn in, hugging the white line, repeat.

Conquering a New Track

By Ryan Maker
(4 x Modified Australian National Champion)

Arriving at a new track which you haven't driven a lap on, can be quite intimidating, especially when the locals are already flying around. Don't let it get to you, just start slow and do your own thing.

First, pick your driver's stand position. Everyone is different, but I like to position myself relative to the centre of the track, which is not necessarily the centre of the driver's stand. If there's a particular part of the track I'm struggling to see or drive, then I may move 1–2m towards that section for a better view. It's amazing how different a track can look depending on where you stand!

Take a close look at each of the curbs. Sometimes a track will use various curb sizes in different parts of the track. It is important to know which curbs you can drive over and which are too high. Also, take note of each curbs white painted line. Sometimes the white line will be painted on the curb and on others it will be on the asphalt. If the white line is on the track, then you know you can drive up to and on the white line. If it is on the curb, then you know you need to maintain a small gap to stay off the curb. Some tracks also have raised white lines due to the thick paint used. If the paint is thick and traction is high, it can almost act as a curb/bump and cause traction rolling, so pay close attention to it at every track you drive on.

Initially, you should focus solely on your driving; ignore car setup until you've learnt the track. I make sure I can drive for five minutes without mistakes before changing my car setup. Start slowly and don't drive too fast, as you need to learn the confines of the track. A track can sometimes drive very differently to how it looks, and sections that look easy can sometimes be hard to navigate.

Once you're up to speed (usually 3–4 battery packs) you can start to look at your car setup. Don't get too carried away. Make sure you stay close to the normal setup that you run at home (assuming it's a similar track).

Make changes, if they don't work, then change them back. Something I see many people doing is making a change, and if they don't know if it's better or not, they just leave it. Bad move! If something isn't an obvious step in the right direction, then you should change it back to what you know. Otherwise, you will end up on some crazy setup that you have no idea how to fine-tune once racing starts.

Use your practice sessions wisely and, if possible, go out on the track when it isn't too busy. Use old tyres at the start when you are learning the track, and when the track is at its most "race-like" condition. Later, use new tyres in order to get a feel for the car's full potential at race speed.

You will also need to find an additive that works; you should do this once the track is in good condition. It's often trial and error to find one that comes on nicely at the start of the run and doesn't fade too much by the end. It's also critical how you apply it (for tips on tyres and additives refer to page 151). If you are struggling to find something that works, ask a local fast racer. They've probably tried everything and should be able to point you in the right direction. On some tracks, certain additives only work because all the locals are using it and it's what is on the track.

- Try to get as many runs as possible during the practice day. Familiarise yourself with the facility and track to ensure that you are comfortable to start racing.
- Use the tyre preparation for racing that you developed during practice.
- Use what you learnt during practice and replicate it for racing.
- During racing, don't make any significant changes that you "think" might work.
- Often once the track surface is in good condition, you only need to make very small changes to tune your setup, as the car will be more sensitive.

Perfect Practice Makes Perfect

We can break practice into two types:

- Driving Practice — learning the track and practising: braking, cornering, and acceleration.
- Testing — where you identify areas of the track where your car's handling could be improved, changing the setup and re-testing to see if the change is better or worse.

Experienced drivers will often combine these two types of practice, but when learning, it can be easier to focus on one.

Practice is only useful if done as close to race conditions as possible. If you use tyre additive and tyre warmers at a race meeting, then make sure you do this when practising. If you are practising for an event, then use the same brand and model of tyres for practice that you will use during the event. Otherwise, you may waste your time as your car's grip is likely to be completely different.

Fast cornering takes practice. Identify the racing line you want to take and practice it. Change the setup of your car to make your ideal racing line as easy and fast to drive as possible. It is often easier to focus your practice on getting one or two corners right each lap rather than trying to get every corner perfect. Once you are happy with the corners you've been practising, focus on the next couple of corners. The goal, of course, is to lower your lap times.

Practising the way you will race and focusing on getting one corner right at a time until you can string them all together is "Perfect Practice", hence the title of this section.

form
Driver Etiquette and Traffic

If your car is involved in an incident, you are losing time. This section covers proper driving etiquette and how you can use it to prevent incidents.

The following provides guidance on how to handle common situations when racing:

Lapping

Drivers that are being lapped must give way to the lapping car. The race software may call cars that are about to be lapped when they cross the start/finish line, but of course, the leaders can catch people at other parts of the track. It can sometimes be confusing whether you are being lapped or not. If you are lapping someone and they are not moving aside, then call out "red car lapping blue car", for example, so that the blue car knows the situation. The blue car must allow the red car to pass without blocking them. Of course if you are racing for position and not being lapped then block away.

Staggered Start Passing

Staggered starts for qualifying (also called IFMAR Called starts) are used at most large events and also at some club meetings, create an interesting situation when passing or lapping. This is how it works.

If you wait until your name or car number is called before starting, then it is a staggered start. During staggered start qualifying, you are racing the clock rather than the other cars on the track. Your personal timer starts when you cross the start/finish line for the first time and ends when the race software calls the end of the race plus the lap you are on (always keep going until your name, or car number, is called as finished). That other cars are on the track is irrelevant to you; it is only done to save time. Of course, if someone blocks you in this situation, then that can hurt your qualifying. You must not block people in staggered start qualifying. If someone catches you, then let them pass. Note that with staggered starts you should let people pass if they are quicker than you, whether they are lapping you or not.

How to Pass

How to let other cars pass deserves some discussion. When you are learning to drive, it's difficult to move out of someone's way without crashing. The best way to let someone pass is to go slightly wide at a corner. Sudden changes in speed or direction can cause a crash. Slowing down suddenly might cause the passing car to crash into the back of you. If you let the person know when you will go slightly wide, then they can take advantage of it to pass. If the lapping car is Blue, then say "pass me on the inside Blue car at the next corner" or simply "inside Blue car". If you know the person's name, then use it to be even clearer e.g., "inside Jim". The passing racer will appreciate it, and it will have the least impact on your own qualifying time.

Resolving Disputes

You may have heard the term "hacked" or "taken out", for example, "he hacked me". This slang means the person feels someone crashed into them. If there is a racing incident that affects you, why not speak to the person involved immediately after the race? Racers who are new to the hobby sometimes need guidance on what is acceptable behaviour. As long as this guidance is provided in a positive and friendly manner, then most of the time, the person will change their behaviour. Sometimes people get angry in the heat of the moment. Walking away and trying to talk to them later, when they've cooled down, often works. If the behaviour continues, then notify the Race Director.

After a Crash

If you cause an accident, then the correct behaviour is to wait for that person to continue before you continue. An apology after the race never hurts either. We should all be aware that the speeds and distances involved mean that mistakes happen, and that's racing. It's how we handle it that matters.

Hitting Someone From Behind

If you hit someone from behind, then it's always your fault. You control where your car is at any given time on the track. If the car in front brakes unexpectedly, then that may well cause an incident, but that you ran into the back of them is your fault. If you are coming up behind someone you've never raced with before, then it pays to be more cautious.

Marshals

If your car has left the track or is on its roof, then hopefully a marshal will assist you as soon as possible.

If a marshal doesn't see your car is in trouble, then a single call of "Marshal" is acceptable to draw their attention to it. Remember that if you hadn't crashed a marshal wouldn't be necessary, so treat marshals with the respect they deserve.

The marshal's priorities are their safety and to not cause issues for the drivers who haven't crashed. So marshals will not rush in front of other cars on the track to get to your car. Nor should you expect them to fix any issues with your car.

When your car is back on the track, do not pull out in front of another car. Wait until there is a gap.

Chapter 3

The Build

SPEED SECRETS

Introduction

In 2016 I wrote my book **Speed Secrets**, detailing everything I knew at that time about car preparation and setup. Four years on and I have updated everything with the latest tools and tips. You will see my Speed Secrets in the next three chapters and throughout this book.

We all race to enjoy ourselves and improve our skills and speed on the track. First things first, you need to be able to drive. Don't get me wrong; no amount of setup knowledge will make a C-Main driver win the A-Main overnight. However, it is a lot easier to improve your skills when you have a predictable, fast car. I'm sure there is a lot of talent wasted in this hobby when decent drivers become sick of driving a poorly performing car and have no idea how to fix it. Sure, you need to have decent equipment, but you don't need to have the best in order to be up the front consistently, you just need to know how to use what you have to its full potential.

The first step to improving your lap times and confidence on the track is to build the car correctly. There's nothing better than opening a fresh kit — lap times in a box! Well ... only if you build it correctly. I hear so many racers say "I just need to give this new kit a few club days to iron out any bugs, wear in all the components and get it up to speed with my current car" — I can tell you, if this is the case, you are doing it wrong! Every brand new car I've ever put on the track has come within one-tenth of a second per lap of my previous car, or even faster on its first ever run. If you build the car correctly, it should be at optimum performance immediately. I will help you find the extra performance you have been looking for.

First of all, you can't achieve this result by simply following instruction manuals. Some parts of the car are relatively straight forward and can be assembled using the instructions. However, there are many aspects along the way that require extra attention. If you ever wondered what the pros do, you're about to find out! They are all great drivers, don't get me wrong, but how can World Champions end up two finals down from where they finished in recent years? The driver is just as good as when they won, or near enough. This proves that having a perfect car can make a world of difference.

Nobody makes it to the top based on sheer talent alone, you need to work for it, you need to put in the hours at the workbench, and the hours at the track. If I told you how much time pro drivers spend working on their cars, you probably wouldn't believe me. If you think you're putting in too much time, you're not. There's always someone out there working harder than you, so keep pushing the boundaries and keep pushing your limits and the results will come.

Of course, to follow my build advice, you don't have to have a brand new kit. Strip down your current car completely and follow the build that way.

I admire your commitment and wish you all the best in your future races. If you have questions, please feel free to email me or stop me for a chat at the track.

- ✓ 4 x Modified Australian National Champion
- ✓ 10 x State Champion
- ✓ 17th at the 2016 IFMAR World Championship

Ryan Maker

ryan@rcmaker.com.au — rcmaker.com.au — facebook.com/rcmaker1

Author's note:

Ryan Maker is one of the most accomplished drivers in Australasia. He owns RC Maker, a manufacturer of many unique RC products and a distributor of racing kits and parts. Many of the products Ryan refers to in these pages are available from rcmaker.com.au.

The Rules

People are often puzzled when they copy a pro driver's setup and it doesn't really work at all, even though the setup is suited to their track conditions. Here's what they do differently:

Rule 1: No setup will give you an edge unless the car is mechanically perfect.

I cannot stress this rule enough. Attention to detail! What do I mean by that? Isn't following the instructions assembling the car correctly? Not at all! The tolerances of RC parts are close, but never perfect, no matter which manufacturer. I will explain exactly how to do this, and you will learn the steps all top race teams and drivers go through to perform at their best every race.

Rule 2: Take your time; being pedantic is a necessity.

The best of the best take days to build their car and hours to mount body shells. It's this attention to detail that makes the difference, so that the car will perform perfectly. This is what the pros do — and it's what you should do too. Just because you may not be a professional driver, doesn't mean you can't get the most out of your equipment and give yourself the best chance you can of achieving your goals at races.

Rule 3: Do your own thing, never let others influence your decisions and methods.

You don't see Ronald Völker taking setup tips off Marc Rheinard. There are very good reasons for this. First, the obvious ones; they don't have the same car and are direct competitors, so naturally they won't be trying to make each other faster. However, the most important reason is they each have their own procedures and understanding of building, setting up and maintaining their cars. This is generated from their experience, and due to the fact they both win races, it proves there is not only one way to do things. I urge you to stick to your guns, practice what you have learnt in the pits and on the track. Pros do their own thing and it works!

The Build

Preparation

"The will to win is important, the will to prepare is vital" — Joe Paterno

Plastic Parts

When I build a kit, I will prepare all the plastic parts first. This is all the suspension components and diff gears, body posts, shock plastics, the lot. The first stage of this is trimming off any extra moulding flashing or extra plastic bits from where the part was broken off the plastic tree.

Pivot Pins

Next, prepare your 3mm inner and outer suspension pins. Use the suspension pins that you'll be using in your car (if you are using titanium from the manufacturer, don't do this process with the standard steel ones).

Most touring cars on the market have four suspension arms, and each of these has two pivot pins. One pivot pin connecting the arm to the chassis and one connecting the arm to the hub (to a C-hub at the front or a rear hub at the rear).

One at a time, test fit each of these eight pivot pins by sliding it inside its suspension arm. The pivot pin must spin in the plastic arm with absolutely no resistance.

To achieve this, you will usually need to use a 3mm arm reamer to remove small amounts of material from the suspension armhole. Remove a small amount of material and re-test. You may need to repeat this process several times, ensuring that you don't remove too much material. Excessive arm reaming can lead to an oversized hole which causes slop resulting in premature wear.

If you don't have a 3mm arm-reamer, I highly recommend buying one. Alternatively, you could use a small round file.

Next, test fit the pin in the hub and ream as necessary so that the pin can spin with absolutely no resistance.

Repeat this process for all eight suspension armholes and four hub holes.

Carbon Fibre Parts

Next up are the carbon fibre parts. This is a personal preference which doesn't particularly affect the car's performance; however, it is always nice to do it prior to assembling your masterpiece. I sand the edges of the chassis, top deck and shock towers so they aren't sharp — carbon splinters aren't nice! You can also seal the chassis with super glue. This has a very slight effect on stiffening the carbon, however it is quite small and just depends how much time you want to invest.

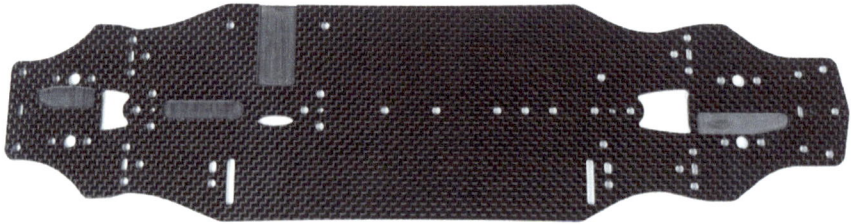

Personally, I change my chassis every few months, so gluing it is not necessary to prolong its life. If you intend keeping the chassis on the car for the duration of its life, I would definitely recommend sealing it. Also ensure you sand the battery tape slots, the sharp carbon can easily cut your battery tape.

Driveshaft Lubrication

Your driveshafts will do a lot of work, and should be inspected prior to assembly. Ensure that the clips on the front DCJ's are installed properly and rear clips are installed on the CVD. Where clips are not used, the grub screw holding the pin should be installed using Loctite and tightened firmly.

Prepare any moving joints with lubrication prior to assembly. Depending on the manufacturer, they will come assembled with some sort of lube. I highly recommend the Muchmore Racing Joint Lube. This lube is quite thick and sticky, and doesn't spin off the joints when they are moving. You want to apply the joint lube to the front DCJ driveshaft joints, front spool outdrives, and rear driveshaft joint. Make sure you get a nice amount of lube on all moving parts of the joint. If there's any excess, just wipe it up with a paper towel.

Screw Tension

Many people don't consider the proper screw tension and do things up way too tight! I urge you to drop your hulk-like screw tightening habits from now on and do things up snugly on everything except for the drivetrain. It's hard to describe how tight this is, but if you hold the wrench with your fingers only (no palm) and do it as tight as possible, that'll be about right. Try and replicate that tension tightening a screw normally. You can eventually train your hand to be like a torque wrench, as having a consistent screw tension is very important. Basically, this tension applies for screwing carbon fibre to alloy or plastic. If there is no carbon fibre involved, then you can tighten it as much as you feel necessary. What we are trying to do is keep the pressure of the carbon fibre consistent against the alloy or plastic. This has a substantial effect on the flex of the car. However, for steering and drivetrain components (especially spool cups), you can go to town and do them up tight and use Loctite if you wish.

Tighten screws using the following pattern to minimise the chance of tweaking the chassis:

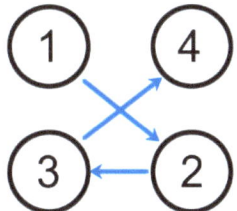

For more information on Tweak refer to page *163*.

Chassis Assembly

Before you start, choose a starting setup. This may be the manufacturer's default setup, one you've used before, or something else. For example, how much rear toe-in should you set when building the car? Yes, you can change this later but by having a starting setup to refer to you can prevent having to change things during the Initial Setup phase. Read the Initial Setup Introduction on page 70 to select a starting setup before you assemble your chassis.

Mostly, you can refer to the manufacturer's instruction manual in order to assemble the car correctly. Make sure you apply **Rule 1: No setup will give you an edge unless the car is mechanically perfect**. Focus on the details. The objective is to make every moving component perfectly free, with minimum slop.

Suspension Components

I always assemble the suspension components first, as they are the absolute pivotal point on the car.

Start by installing the suspension blocks and suspension arms on the chassis. One oversight I often see is people not tightening their suspension blocks perpendicular to the chassis. If this mistake is made, it will cause different amounts of lateral movement (play) in the suspension arm between the blocks on each side. The aim here is to make the blocks perpendicular to the chassis, while tightening them in a way that ensures that the suspension arm is pivoting with absolutely no resistance.

Ensure there is minimal forward and back movement (play) in the arm between the suspension blocks. If you push the front and rear block together whilst tightening and there is still slop in the arm, you may need to consider adding a 0.1 or 0.2mm shim on both the left and right arm. What happens to one side must always be replicated on the opposite side. Keep adjusting until you have less than 0.1mm of lateral movement on both arms, so they are both moving the same amount, and your arms are perfectly free and moving up and down with zero resistance.

You can then install the hubs on the arms. I like to do this without the driveshafts installed, as the driveshafts increase the mass and help the hubs pivot, possibly hiding any minute binding between the hub and the suspension arm. If there is any binding between any of these parts, and the suspension pins are perfectly free, then the fit of the plastics is too tight. You can take a small file and remove some material from the edge of the arm or hub (you can file either just ensure you keep it consistent). Conversely, if there is any excess movement you can attempt to fit a 0.1mm shim to reduce the movement. If you do this, ensure that the extra 0.1mm shim isn't causing any binding.

I know this may sound overboard, but I assure you, nothing I am telling you is overboard! These are the things most people don't pay attention to, and this is what will help you get the edge.

Lower Bulkheads and Chassis

Once all the main suspension components are installed, we can look at assembling the bulkheads. This is an important process which, if done incorrectly, can cause tweaks in the chassis. Start by installing the four main lower bulkheads, but don't fully tighten the screws.

If your car's bulkheads are keyed into the chassis i.e., the bulkhead has a lug which fits a slot in the chassis, then you can go ahead and tighten the screws (Loctite is recommended) and the bulkheads will be correctly aligned.

Otherwise, I recommend a bulkhead alignment tool for your particular chassis, such as the Vigor brand. This tool is an alloy bar as long as the chassis which fits between the bulkheads and allows you to align them perfectly front and rear, whilst also making them square with the chassis. You can proceed to tighten the bulkhead screws whilst applying pressure to the bulkheads against the bar. After the process is completed, you can remove the bar leaving you with four perfectly square bulkheads. This is the foundation for the car and will ensure no tweaking in later assembly.

Next, attach the motor mount bulkhead (you can't do this with the bulkhead alignment tool in place as the motor mount attaches to the centre of the car).

Drivetrain

Now it's time to assemble the parts required for the drivetrain.

The centre layshaft and front spool can be built following the instruction manual.

Gear Diff Assembly

The gear diff is an essential part of the car's handling. A smooth, precise diff will feel noticeably better on the track than a notchy diff. This assembly can be slightly different between manufacturers; however, the key elements remain the same. First, ensure that the diff outdrives spin freely inside the diff housing before doing any greasing or assembly. If there is any binding, you may need to use a drill bit to enlarge the hole ever so slightly. I recommend doing this by hand slowly, to not remove too much material. Normally this is unnecessary; however, due to the moulding process, sometimes flashing can remain there and cause slight binding which we can remove with the drill bit. Ensure the diff gears and crossbar you prepared earlier are perfect, with no excess material. I like to very lightly sand the back of all the gears, just to ensure that they will sit perfectly flat when inside the diff. I use Associated Green Slime between the diff outdrives and case, and also on all the O-rings in the diff.

Assemble the diff as per the manufacturer's instructions, ensuring each part has a perfect fit when assembling. I like to fill the diff half full before inserting the spider gears; this ensures that the oil is down inside all crevices of the diff and that there are no pockets of air trapped under the spider gears. Insert the spider gears and press down on the cross brace with a wrench to seat them. You can start with the instruction manual's recommendation on viscosity. For advice on when to use different viscosity oils refer to page *115*.

Fill the diff up with your desired oil to the top of the spider gears. I always overfill the diff and have excess oil seep out rather than under filling. My testing has found an underfilled diff will feel quite inconsistent when it is hot and can thin out badly during the run. The larger volume of oil stays more consistent throughout the run.

Once you have the other half of the diff attached, tighten the diff screws in a star pattern, so it seats properly against the O-ring and gasket. If your diff is slightly notchy, don't stress; it is one of those parts of the car that need to run in and will be smooth after a few runs.

Belt Tension

You can then install your drivetrain into the bulkheads. Achieving the correct belt tension can be difficult as there is no top deck installed yet. Just set it to the default manufacturer's recommendations to start with, and it can be tuned later. Belt tension is quite important:

- For a **rear-mount motor**, I run the front slightly tighter than the rear due to the extra length on the front belt. However, if your car doesn't use a centre motor mount post, you may need to run the rear reasonably tight as well. This is due to the extra front-to-back flex in the car, which will loosen the rear belt under acceleration and allow it to skip.

- For a **mid-mount motor**, I use belt tension which is almost equal front-to-rear. I make the rear belt one notch tighter as it is subject to slightly greater acceleration forces.

For further information on Belt Tension refer to page *96*.

Also, pay close attention to the diff height, the eccentric holders can be adjusted on most cars to raise or lower the drivetrain. For now, install them as per the instruction manual. For details on how this setting affects handling refer to Diff Height on page *118*.

Wheel Hexes and Drive Shafts

Install all of the drive shafts into the hubs and fasten the wheel hex. Ensure there is no binding when a wheel is tightened onto the hex; conversely, that there isn't too much slop. If binding occurs, you may need to lightly sand the back of the wheel hex to release some pressure from the bearing. If there is too much play, then you can add a 0.1mm x 4mm ID shim. Just check that adding this doesn't bind the hex. Re-attach and tighten the wheel to check that the hex remains free after adding the shim.

Pay very close attention to the resistance on the wheel, often the big wheel will hide any minute binding, so double check that it also feels smooth and free once you've taken the wheel off.

Repeat this process for all four corners of the car. Don't install the wheels, you are just checking to see the tolerances.

Ensure that the rear c-blade is moving freely on the drive shaft pin. If not, you may need to use a 2mm drill bit to slightly enlarge the hole in the blade. We want to make sure all moving parts are perfectly free with no binding.

Upper Bulkheads and Chassis Finishing

Install the upper bulkheads and shock towers as per the manufacturer's instructions. Make sure you tighten the upper bulkheads and shock towers square to the lower bulkheads. You can also now install the top deck and belt tensioner, and make the turnbuckles for the camber links.

When installing the top deck, ensure the car is on a perfectly flat surface; apply pressure to both of the shock towers equally whilst tightening the screws. It is important to make sure these screws are tightened as per Screw Tension on page 50. Tighten them in the following order; the front two, rear two, front two, rear two, and lastly the centre motor mount screw if applicable.

Once that's done, you can install all the camber link ball studs and make up the turnbuckles. When assembling the turnbuckles, I always like to have the right/left thread facing the same way throughout the car, so you know that forward is tighten/loosen on the whole car or vice versa. This takes the guesswork out of adjusting camber. You can set the lengths to the factory default; we can fine-tune these when we do the main setup on the car later, so don't be too concerned about making these exactly as per the manual.

One important thing to note is how the ball cups pivot on the ball studs. They should be perfectly free with no binding at all. If there is binding, a trick is to lightly squeeze the ball cup with pliers. If that doesn't work, you can use a heat gun or cigarette lighter to heat it up quickly whilst it's on the ball stud and move it around. With these all popped on and free, you should have a perfectly free moving, slop free suspension.

If you've got this far, your car is already more precise than 90% of the people you are racing against at your club!

Shock Absorbers

Time for another one of the most important aspects of the car, the shock absorbers. These are probably the hardest thing on the car to get perfect, but are critical to ensuring the car handles perfectly on the track. All manufacturers' shocks are different, but work in a similar way. First, gather the shock parts you prepared earlier and double-check you haven't missed any excess material on any of the plastic parts. The most important are the bushings and pistons, as these are crucial to a smoothly functioning shock. Make sure the pistons are all drilled properly, and there is no excess material blocking the holes. Also, pay close attention to which direction the instruction manual recommends you place the groove on the piston. Some manufacturers place the groove upwards, whilst some place it down.

When assembling the bottom part of the shock, ensure you lubricate the O-ring first; a dry O-ring can be damaged very easily by the shock shaft threads. When assembling the shock piston and shock shaft, the key is to fit the piston so it has no movement up or down. It doesn't particularly matter if the piston spins on the shaft or not with the C-clips installed, but ensuring there is no vertical movement in the piston is crucial. You can adjust this by using 0.1mm shims under the piston to ensure you get each one perfect.

When inserting the shaft through the body and O-ring, I like to put a drop of shock oil on the tip, to further lubricate the O-ring and prevent damage. When screwing the plastic shock bottom ball cup on, ensure you are screwing it on straight and not crooked, as this can make the shock retainer sit on an angle. The manufacturer will recommend a shock length setting, usually between the bottom of the shock body and the top of the shock bottom. Use callipers to get this internal measurement exactly as per the manufacturer's recommendation. Altering this length influences handling and is a tuning option (refer to page 106).

All manufacturers' shocks require different techniques to obtain the perfect rebound (usually described in the manual). Some people also like to drill a 1mm hole in the plastic top cap to relieve the pressure above the bladder, in order to achieve zero rebound. I personally don't like this idea, as it doesn't allow the shock to work naturally, and a natural shock has rebound. However, this is my personal preference.

When I build my shocks, I use about 3mm of rebound front and rear, and try to make them as even as I can. Within 0.5mm is usually good enough. For the majority of shocks, you need to fill the oil to the top, pump the piston up and down a few times, ensuring that it doesn't go above the oil height. I like to use Muchmore shock oil, but you can use whatever brand shock oil is used by most racers with the same brand car as yours. This way, it is a lot easier to compare setups. If you are building brand new shocks, after pumping the piston, you may need to top up the oil as the oil takes up the surface area under the piston.

Let the shocks sit for as long as they need until all the air is gone. You can also use a shock pump which creates a vacuum and speeds up this process, however, it can suck air through the bottom O-ring and do more harm than good if pumped too hard.

To set rebound, push the shaft up to where the thread starts on the shock shaft, gently insert the bladder into the top of the shock body and tap down on it gently. You will see oil seeping out from under the bladder. Keep tapping down until all the excess oil is removed; don't be in a rush to do this process, you can take your time.

The next part is really important; whilst the shaft is still up, screw the shock top down onto the body, ensuring you don't disturb the shock bladder. Keep tightening until the shock top is as tight as it will go whilst holding the shaft in the same position. You should have the perfect shock with no air, and a little rebound. If there is too much rebound, you can loosen the cap two turns, push the shock up to the thread again (don't go too high or you'll suck in air) and hold it whilst tightening the cap again. It should slightly reduce rebound every time you repeat this process. If the shock has air in it, you may have either expelled too much oil from under the bladder, disturbed the bladder when locating and tightening the top cap, or pushed the shaft up too high when setting rebound. For more on rebound, refer to page *111*.

Once all four are perfect, you can prepare them by inserting the balls into the cups and attaching the shock spring with the retainer. Put them aside as we will attach them later.

Roll Bars

It's roll bar time! It's fascinating how many people don't appreciate the role these play on the car or understand how to assemble them correctly. This will teach you, once and for all, how to set up your roll bars to be active, de-tweaked and free.

First, check that the roll bar wire is flat; you can do this by putting it on a flat surface, checking there are no twists or bends. If it is not perfectly flat the entire way around the bar, then you may need to lightly bend the wire in order to straighten it. You must do this for both the front and rear bars first, before assembling anything.

Depending on your brand of car, your roll bar system will pivot on bearings, or rotate inside a plastic holder with a grub screw to set the tension.

- With the **bearing system**, installing the roll bar on the bulkheads is fairly straight forward; the biggest thing here is to ensure that the roll bar is located perfectly in the centre of the bulkheads.

- With a **holder and grub screw**, you need to tighten the grub screws until they just restrict the roll bars movement, from there you can back both of them off to ensure the roll bar has perfectly free movement with zero slop. To achieve this, you will need to back each grub screw off in 1/16 of a turn increments to get it absolutely spot on. At the end of this process, your roll bar should rotate up and down with no resistance, and have no slop between the wire and the grub screws.

Next comes the installation of the roll bar linkages; the crucial element in having a perfectly functioning roll bar system. When you assemble the linkages, ensure they are the same length. I like to set the length not by the manual, but so that the wire is parallel with the ground, with the car sitting off the bench. Just make sure your droop is correct before you check this (you can set it now by referring to page 70), and you should come up with a measurement that you can always replicate.

Next, ensure that the ball cups are perfectly free on the balls connecting to both the arm and the roll bar end. You can check by individually popping the top and bottom ball on, checking that the linkage pivots with no binding. If there is binding, sometimes squeezing the ball cup with pliers, or heating it up quickly with a heat gun or cigarette lighter can be all it takes to free it up.

Once everything is connected and perfect, you can continue building. We will come back to de-tweaking the roll bar linkages later, once the car is all set up and all angles are correct.

Steering Rack

Next, you will build your steering assembly. I find many people are really particular about this aspect of the car, which isn't a bad thing, but getting your steering 100% slop free is not a necessity. I often build my steering out of the box, and most importantly check that it's perfectly free; a little slop is nothing to worry about. You can choose whether to Loctite the screws or not, I never have, but I also check my screws regularly; this is a personal preference. If you are using Loctite, ensure it doesn't go inside the bearings as it could seize them.

Once installed, check that everything moves freely, including the steering arms. If not, disconnect the ball cups to check which aspect is binding, you may need to use the lighter or pliers to loosen the ball cup as previously mentioned. You can do your link lengths to the manufacturer's recommendations; just ensure that both turnbuckles are facing the same way and that you make both links the same length.

Servo

Next up we will install the servo. There are a few ways of doing this on different car brands, but most of the leading manufacturers now use a floating servo mount. The first thing to note is that you want your servo to be up as high as possible on the mount, so it isn't touching the chassis and interfering with the flex of the car. In terms of fixing the servo to the servo mount, I recommend using a specific locating washer such as these RC Maker ones pictured below. 1up Racing also make a good one. They stop the tabs on the servo from spreading due to over-tightening and allow the servo to be fixed firmly as the inner washer fits perfectly inside the servo tab, unlike a standard 3mm screw.

I like to space the servo forward if room permits; this will free up room for your electronics. A great tip is to lightly sand the bottom of the mount where it contacts the chassis. Use fairly course wet and dry sandpaper (400 grit or similar). This ensures that your servo mount won't shift in a crash. Scuffing this will allow it to grip to the shiny carbon surface and ensure it doesn't move in slight knocks.

Finding a good servo horn is very important. I don't like to use servo savers or plastic servo horns, because I find they can make the car feel lethargic and sometimes cause slight understeer. An alloy horn is far more direct, and has no flex, leading to improved steering response.

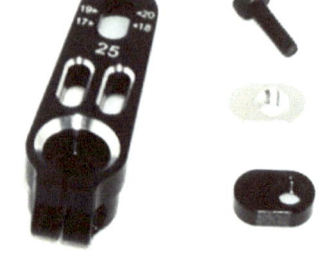

Which servo horn you use depends on the car, but for most leading brands, 16–20mm centre to centre height is a good starting point. Personally, I use an MR33 servo horn (shown above); it is the perfect length and adjustable so you can use the setting which works best with your car. Hudy also have a great range of servo horns varying in length and offset.

Once you find the perfect servo horn, you can sit it on the servo and lightly screw it in. A good trick to roughly centre the steering servo and horn (without powering up the servo), is to turn the servo all the way clockwise and put the servo horn parallel to the servo case.

Next, lightly screw on the servo horn ball and attach it to the ball cup linking the steering servo and steering assembly. When the steering is centred, the steering linkage should be at 90 degrees to the servo horn (and therefore parallel to the front shock tower). Depending on your chassis brand and servo horn, you will probably need to add shims between the ball and the horn to achieve this angle (shown in green below). This gives the steering a linear feel which is what we want. If the steering linkage is angled then the steering feel will be progressive.

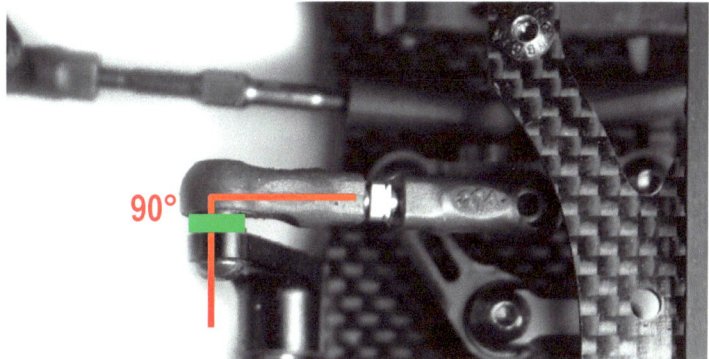

When you turn the wheels, the angle may no longer be 90 degrees, and the steering linkage may no longer be parallel to the shock tower. That's ok; it's not relevant.

After achieving this, you can do the ball up tightly. I also like to use Loctite as it is constantly moving and rarely needs to be disassembled.

Don't screw your servo horn on to the servo too tightly just yet; we will set this up later.

Finishing Touches

Your car should be almost finished. We just need to assemble the bumper and body posts, and we can begin setting it up. There's no rocket science to this, assemble as per the manual. Don't cut the body posts just yet, we can do that later when mounting the body. When you have completed the bumper assembly, don't mount it to the car; it is a lot easier to set the car up perfectly without the bumper.

Congratulations on assembling a perfect car! What we have achieved to this point is a solid foundation in which all components will function perfectly. With everything straight and precise, your car can perform at its peak.

Elements

Notice that I've broken the car down into its elements. Most people think of the car as just one functioning body, but I always like to break it down into the different sections:

Drivetrain:
Front spool, rear diff, centre layshaft, belts, DCJs and CVDs.

Chassis:
Bottom deck, top deck, bulkheads, suspension mounts, shock towers, steering rack.

Suspension:
All moving parts, suspension plastics, camber links, roll bars, shock absorbers.

By doing this, it simplifies setup and maintenance and improves your understanding of how everything works together. I encourage you to be aware of the separate components and feel comfortable working on your car at, and away from, the track.

Electronics

I hate to say it, but this is where many people get lazy. However, this can be the difference between a car that looks ok, and a car that is beautifully presented. Will it make it go faster? Debatable, but everyone should feel proud of their car. It's like trying to work in a dirty office; it's never as nice as a perfectly clean office where you know where everything is.

Mid-motor Mount

Rear-motor Mount

Please take your time installing your electronics. I realise you're not all electricians with machine-like soldering abilities, but you don't need to be. Here are a few steps to help you layout your electronics in any conventional car.

Your servo is already in. Now I suggest you also install your motor with the correct pinion gear (page 127), set your gear mesh (page 243) and tighten your motor. You have now identified the space you have to work with for your receiver and ESC. As long as you don't have electronics from the 1980s, you should easily be able to fit both components neatly in the space. Mount your receiver with about a 1mm gap to your servo. You don't want it to be hard up against it, or it could impede your floating servo's flex characteristics. I like to use good quality double-sided tape when mounting my electronics. This ensures they stay in place and are easy enough to remove when you want to replace the electronics or change chassis. I use MR33 clear double-sided tape (similar to 3M/Scotch), as it peels off in one piece and sticks like nothing else!

Shortening Wires

I recommend shortening your servo wire, so there is no extra length when you plug it in. You can do this in one of two ways:

Option 1: If you're good at soldering and have a good soldering iron with a small tip, take the back off your servo and unsolder the wires from the tabs. I like to replace the standard coloured wires with black insulated servo leads available from RC Maker. This will most likely void the manufacturer's warranty, so just make sure you are competent in doing this. If you want to be really tricky and neat, you can spin the rear case around and solder the wire onto the board from the other direction. It routes the lead out the other side of the servo, but be really careful you get the polarities correct! I often mark the board with a + and – so I know.

Option 2: The safer option is to buy a crimping tool and spare servo plugs. Cut the servo lead and crimp new pins on to the leads creating a new plug.

I can't stress enough when using either of these methods, make sure you note the orientation of the wires! A good idea is to take a photo before you start work, so you know exactly how it was beforehand.

When shortening wires remember, "Measure twice, cut once" and double-check both ends of the wire to ensure it is the correct polarity/type. There's nothing more annoying than cutting your wire only to find you've measured from the "B" pole on the ESC to the "A" pole on the motor, and your wire won't reach the correct location!

Mounting the ESC

If your ESC is not brand new, I recommend installing new battery and motor wires to make everything look nice in your shiny new car. Leave them all quite lengthy, obviously leaving more length on your battery wires than the motor wires. I always use Muchmore Black 12 AWG wire for Modified (14 AWG for Stock and 16 AWG for 21.5 turn). This is super heavy duty wire that will never let you down and looks nice and stealth too. Don't worry about colour coding them or anything; we can identify them on the ESC and also by what length we make them, so it's obvious which outputs go to which inputs.

If you are pedantic like me, you can also shorten the receiver wire coming out of the ESC, using either of the two options you used for shortening the servo wire. Depending on what ESC you have, you will need to find a place for the capacitor.

For a **mid-mount motor**, secure it between the ESC and the rear bulkhead.

If you are using a **rear-mount motor**, you can either put the capacitor between the ESC and motor, or if it's small enough like my Muchmore Fleta Pro V2 capacitor (below), double-sided tape it to the side of the ESC, between the top deck and the bottom of the front belt (as pictured below). Seems risky, but I assure you it isn't, as long as you use quality double-sided tape!

You can now stick your ESC in place. In terms of orientation, modern ESCs are installed with the output wires all facing the motor. If you are in a blinky (non-timing) class, make sure the blinking ESC light can easily be seen by a scrutineer.

Ensure that no part of the ESC is touching the top deck. However, for balance purposes, you don't want it more than 2mm away. You want the ESC mounted as centrally as possible for most cars, without it hitting the top deck.

Left-to-right Weight Balance

You should check the balance of the car with all electronics fitted. If you are using a heavy battery, you may need to mount the ESC further from the chassis centreline in order to balance your car. For tips on balancing your car refer to page 157. Make sure you can access the on/off switch easily and plug the ESC's cable into the receiver.

Soldering

Starting with your motor wires, cut and solder them one at a time. This way you can line them up into a nice loop, making sure they are the correct length. Cut each to the right length, so it reaches the correct pole.

I like to face the battery plugs to the rear of the car. Lipo batteries are normally lighter at the end which has the plugs, so this positions the weight further forward in the car. But this is a tuning option, to move battery weight rearward then place the battery plugs towards the front. Refer to page 95 for a description of how this affects handling.

For the battery wires I like to make a nice loop over the belt (or run them under the top deck if space permits), but make sure that the inside battery plug wire is short enough so it can't possibly reach the other polarity. This will stop you plugging your battery wires in reverse; probably the number one annoying mistake an RC racer can make! You can also put some red heat shrink on the positive wire or 1up Racing make a nice set of identifiers (see photo).

Motor Cooling Fan

Next, you can install a motor cooling fan (normally in front of the motor when mid-mounted or behind the motor when rear-mounted). If you can solder your fan wires direct to the + and – outputs on the ESC, then the motor will receive an additional 2.4V (and therefore spin faster and provide more cooling) compared to plugging into the receiver.

A trick for hiding your fan wire is to run it between the motor mount and the motor right down in the corner near the chassis. Most motors will have a bevel which allows you to squeeze the fan wire down in there. However, if it is jamming things, you may have no other choice than to route it over the top of the motor. You can either double-sided tape your fan down, or use a purpose-built mount.

Transponder

I use the very nice mPTX transponder from MRT. You can position this wherever it fits; mine sits nicely on top of my receiver and I install black servo wire, of the correct length, to be stealth! Mylaps also offer a black transponder.

Some racers like to put the transponder at the front of the car for those photo finishes, but this makes the wiring untidy. At beginner speeds, the receiver crosses the finish line about 0.02 of a second after the front bumper. At Modified speeds it's about 0.007 of a second. I've never had my race position affected by the transponder location and would much rather have a tidy wiring installation.

Now your electronics are installed, you can power it all up. Make sure you have a new model on your transmitter. You are now ready to set up the car for its first run!

Chapter 4: Initial Setup

SPEED SECRETS

Initial Setup 4

Introduction

Ryan Maker continues his Speed Secrets, taking you through the Initial Setup steps for your car.

So you've poured hours into building your car and the tolerances of all components are perfect. Now it's time to apply a setup to get your car dialled from the first lap you do around the track. I can't comment too much on different cars' setups. However, if you have never used your car before, then I suggest starting with the kit setup provided by the manufacturer.

Another avenue for more experienced racers is to head to **PetitRC.com**. They have a fantastic setup sheet database for all models. You can find a setup from a team driver for similar track conditions and apply that as a starting point. It may require less fine-tuning than the kit setup.

If you have driven this model of chassis before, or you have just rebuilt your current car, then you can apply the same setup you have developed.

Assuming you have built your car to the setup you've selected, we can progress with setting up the variable aspects of the car such as the wheel angles, droop, ride height, toe-out, steering angles, etc.

Droop

Let's set the droop as we need it to be correct before we set the roll bars. Droop is measured with the shocks on. There are a few methods of measuring the droop; the best and most common is to use 10mm blocks and an appropriate droop gauge. I like to use two, a 1mm stepped one (Muchmore pictured below left) and a 0.2mm increment one (MR33 pictured below right). Your setup sheet will provide you with a droop setting for the front and rear of the car, or you can use a setting you have developed previously. I will talk about droop changes and impact on the cars handling, later.

A typical droop setting is 6mm front, 5mm rear, and is measured under the lowest point of the outside of the arm. Use the droop screw (located in the suspension arm) to adjust the droop by minor increments until the arm is touching the droop gauge perfectly. Screwing anti-clockwise will lessen the number (more droop) while screwing clockwise will increase the number (less droop). You can think of droop as the amount of up travel the suspension has (above ride height).

An important thing to note; different brand tyres may have a different diameter. Therefore when changing them you will need to check and adjust your ride height and droop. For a bigger diameter tyre, we need to increase the droop number and lessen the amount of droop. For a smaller diameter tyre we need to decrease the droop number and increase the amount of droop.

For a step-by-step guide to measuring and setting droop refer to page *119*.

Roll Bars

Now we can move on to the roll bars. This is a tricky one, so read very closely and you will once and for all figure out how to set them.

I assume that you've built the roll bars as described on page *58*, but shocks should be disconnected.

Roll bar tweaks are common in over 90% of RC cars on the track and occur when the roll bar does not affect both sides of the car in the same way. To correct this tweak, we need to alter the length of the roll bar links to counteract any minute imperfection in the roll bar.

First, the car must be on a flat surface. You can use the 10mm droop blocks, or remove them, whichever suits. Use your 1mm increment droop gauge or ride height gauge, whichever suits. You can start on the left or the right side, it doesn't matter. Slide your gauge under the outside of the arm, lifting the arm until the suspension arm on the other side of the car starts to lift. Note that number and make sure it is just lifting; you need to pick the closest number to what is lifting the other side. I often backtrack one number just to check it's not closer to that number.

The rear right suspension arm at the point that the roll bar lifts the rear left suspension arm

Let's say it's the right side, and the opposite side is lifting up at 2. Now check the left side, and let's say it starts lifting up the opposite side at 4. Both sides should lift at the same number so we need to correct this. We can either work on one link solely or work on both links at the same time. I prefer to work on both links to correct big tweaks. While it may sound more difficult, it keeps the roll bar around your desired horizontal position more than altering only one link length.

If it's a very minor tweak, it's fine to only work on one. Since the left side is taking 2mm more to lift up the opposite side than the right side, we would consider this a fairly major tweak, so we would look at adjusting both links. We need to increase the link length on the left side, so that at the same height, it is putting more pressure on the other side to lift up. Let's start by unscrewing ¼ of a turn on the left link. You must re-check both sides, because lengthening one will also affect how quickly the right side now lifts the left side up.

Let's say we check the right again, now it is 2.5 and the left is 3.5, this means we have half corrected the tweak, and need to do exactly what we did again, to make them equal at 3 each side. This is where the two-sided adjustment comes in; instead of lengthening the left link another ¼ of a turn, we will shorten the right link by ¼ of a turn. Effectively, it's the same thing; it's just keeping the roll bar from getting too high. Check that this change has translated, and you can tweak by less than ¼ of a turn if need be to get them perfect. It is a lot of trial and error; it can take up to 20 minutes to get both front and rear perfect. This is such an important aspect of the car's handling, so keep playing and tweaking, trial and error is the best way to become comfortable and competent correcting tweaks. The worst that can happen is that you get confused and need to reset them back to the same length left and right and start again. The best way to master this process is to practise.

Now you can screw your shocks on. Roll bar tweak is the only adjustment you must make without the shocks. For the rest of the setup, shocks are required.

For more information about roll bars refer to page 139.

Servo and Steering Alignment

Time to learn how to set up your steering. Unscrew your servo horn from your servo, turn your radio and car on.

Check that your radio settings are: sub-trim 0, steering trim 0, End Points (EPA) 100% and Dual Rates (D/R) 100%.

The biggest mistake people make with this is making the servo horn at 90 degrees to the servo. The servo horn needs to be at a 90-degree angle to the steering link, not to the servo. This means it must create a right angle with the steering link as pictured. Get it as close as you can by locating the servo horn on the spline with the transmitter on and car powered up. You won't be able to get 90 degrees to the link exactly, but we can fine-tune it with sub trim later.

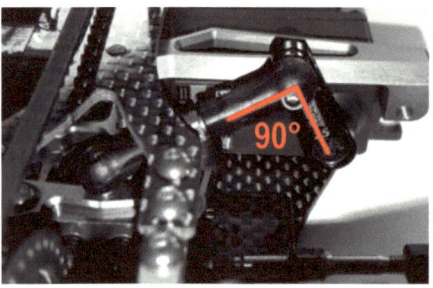

Screw your servo horn on and tighten it heavily; I don't recommend using Loctite as you may not be able to get it off! Once you've done this, we can get the link and the servo horn at exactly 90 degrees using the sub-trim. Ignore what the steering rack is doing; we will get to that next.

You don't have to touch your steering trim or sub-trim from this point, so you can leave that alone. Keep your transmitter on, as we need the steering powered up and centred. The **steering rack** now needs to be located perfectly in the centre; you can often do this by eye-balling the steering rack screws relative to the top deck from a bird's-eye view. Adjust the length of the servo linkage (the link between the servo and the steering rack) so that the steering rack is centred.

Initial Setup 4

After making these changes double-check the steering angles we set during the build are still the same (refer to page 60).

Once the steering rack is centred, we need to turn to the steering links and set toe-out. With your setup station attached, you can set the toe-out by adjusting these links. Shortening the link will increase toe-out, and lengthening the link will decrease toe-out. A typical toe-out setting is 1 degree each side. Make sure you achieve this by ensuring both steering links are the same length. Different length steering links will give different steering angles on inner and outer wheels between left and right. Not what you want on your perfectly built and set up car! For more information on toe-out refer to page 146.

Once this is done, you can set the **steering throw** using the end points (EPA) on your radio. This will be a menu in your transmitter which allows you to adjust the left and right steering locks individually. You want the steering arm to turn until it just brushes the c-hub (as pictured), not flexing it or binding anything, and not so that there's a lot of play in the hub.

Do this for each side individually, and you should find that the numbers on your EPA should be very close to equal either side. If they aren't, it means your steering rack isn't quite centred, servo horn is not quite at 90 degrees, or your main steering links aren't equal lengths. Just go through and find where you could be slightly off, and repeat the process. Ultimately, your left and right EPA should be within 0–5%. For more information on steering throw refer to page *144*.

If you don't like to drive with full steering lock, you can turn it down with the **Dual Rate**. Dual Rate is like EPA, but it adjusts both the left and right side by the same amount, and therefore should be used to increase and decrease the overall steering lock. Doing it this way allows you to always have perfect steering balance left-to-right, with no guessing. Once your EPA is set, you don't need to adjust it unless you have re-adjusted your toe-out setting. If toe-out is adjusted, you must re-do your EPA ensuring Dual Rate is back on 100%.

Ride Height

I like to set the ride height before I set the camber (however, make sure your camber is close), because if your ride height is out by more than 1mm it can throw the camber off. So at least get it close, if not spot on, before you go to set the camber.

Set your ride height on the tyres you'll be using. As tyres wear, they can decrease in diameter, so it is important to check your ride height after every run and every time you change to a different set of tyres.

A fairly typical ride height is 5.0mm front, 5.4mm rear. Good tools for measuring accurately are the Muchmore and MR33 0.2mm increment gauge; the fine increment allows you to make minor adjustments to ride height. I always measure from the very back of the car, and the very front of the car. The front can be difficult, but I slide the ride height gauge in between the bumper and the front suspension arm on the side. This gives a fairly accurate reading, unless your chassis is very worn. If this is the case, you may choose to do it from the opposite side, or find a place near the front or rear in which the chassis is still in good condition. When adjusting your spring preload collars, make sure you do it by the same amount left and right.

For more information on setting ride height refer to page *134*.

Outdoor racing often leaves you with a worn chassis, and this wear occurs primarily on the forward and rear most edges of the chassis. This is where you measure your ride height from, always leaving you with an overstated ride height measurement. Depending on the wear this can be up to 0.4mm, which can make a real difference to the handling of the car! This is a compounding problem, as your ride height is lower than you think, leading to more chassis scraping, and the cycle continues, compounding every run.

The RC Maker gauge (shown below) removes this issue by lengthening the gauge's platforms. The extra reach allows you to access the unworn part of your chassis to achieve an accurate measurement (wear usually only occurs on the outermost part of the chassis). This gauge only provides the most common ride height measurements from 5.0mm to 6.0mm:

Camber

Camber is important and requires a set of tools to adjust accurately. There are two main ways to check camber.

1. **Setup Station** — I can highly recommend the RC Maker, Hudy and Arrowmax Setup Stations as being good quality and very accurate options.

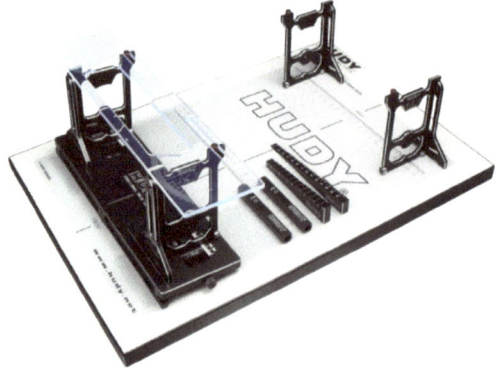

2. **Camber Gauge**, either using setup station wheels or with race ready wheels and tyres. The Muchmore or MR33 camber gauges are good options.

My typical setting for camber is -2 degrees front and rear. This will work in most conditions, however, feel free to set it to whatever you have found to work best in the past. Make sure your camber is measured with the car resting at ride height with the front wheels straight. If you are using a camber gauge, measure in the middle of the wheel where the axle protrudes, and on a flat surface at all times. Ensure you reset the resting ride height by compressing and releasing the suspension before checking the measurement again after adjustments. This is important for both setup station and camber gauge/wheel setup methods.

For more information on camber refer to page *98*.

Tweak

Probably one of the most overlooked and uninformed aspects of setup error is tweak. There are generally two forms of tweak;

1. **Chassis Tweak** — this can be caused by how the top deck, bulkheads and motor mount are tightened. You can ensure your chassis is flat by using a Muchmore Tweak Master to pin your chassis flat while tightening the top deck and bulkheads. You can also press on the shock towers whilst your car is on a flat surface, this will also do the job. Refer to *Testing for Chassis Twist* on page *166*.

2. **Suspension Tweak** — this comes from the suspension and is translated through your shock absorbers. It is noticeable when the chassis is sitting on an angle at ride height, with the shock collars wound down the same amount. This causes the droop (up travel above ride height) to feel different on each side, even though when measured on the droop blocks it is the same. Often people

will never notice this, but it is critical to making your car drive absolutely perfectly. There are several reasons this can occur:

- **Shock tower machining is slightly misaligned** — The shock tower sits on a slight angle or the holes are not perfectly located where the shocks are mounted.

- **Shock springs vary in length** — In a perfect world, shock springs would be identically matched in length. While some company's springs are quite good, some can be out by 0.1–0.3mm, which is enough to throw the ride height and tweak out a lot.

- **Suspension blocks slightly off centre** — In some extreme cases, the suspension blocks may not be drilled in the perfect spot on the chassis, and could cock the arms to one side, effectively making one shock have more distance to cover than the other. We are only talking 0.1–0.2mm, but it all adds up!

In a perfect world, all of this will be absolutely spot on, but often it's not.

We can fix it. Simply follow the detailed steps listed on page *168*.

Finishing Touches

You can now attach your bumper and complete any other finishing touches to your car.

When you first test the car, keep an eye on motor temperature (refer to page *129*).

Congratulations on building an engineering masterpiece! You will now be driving a car with handling that far exceeds anything you've ever driven. You will see results, I can guarantee you that!

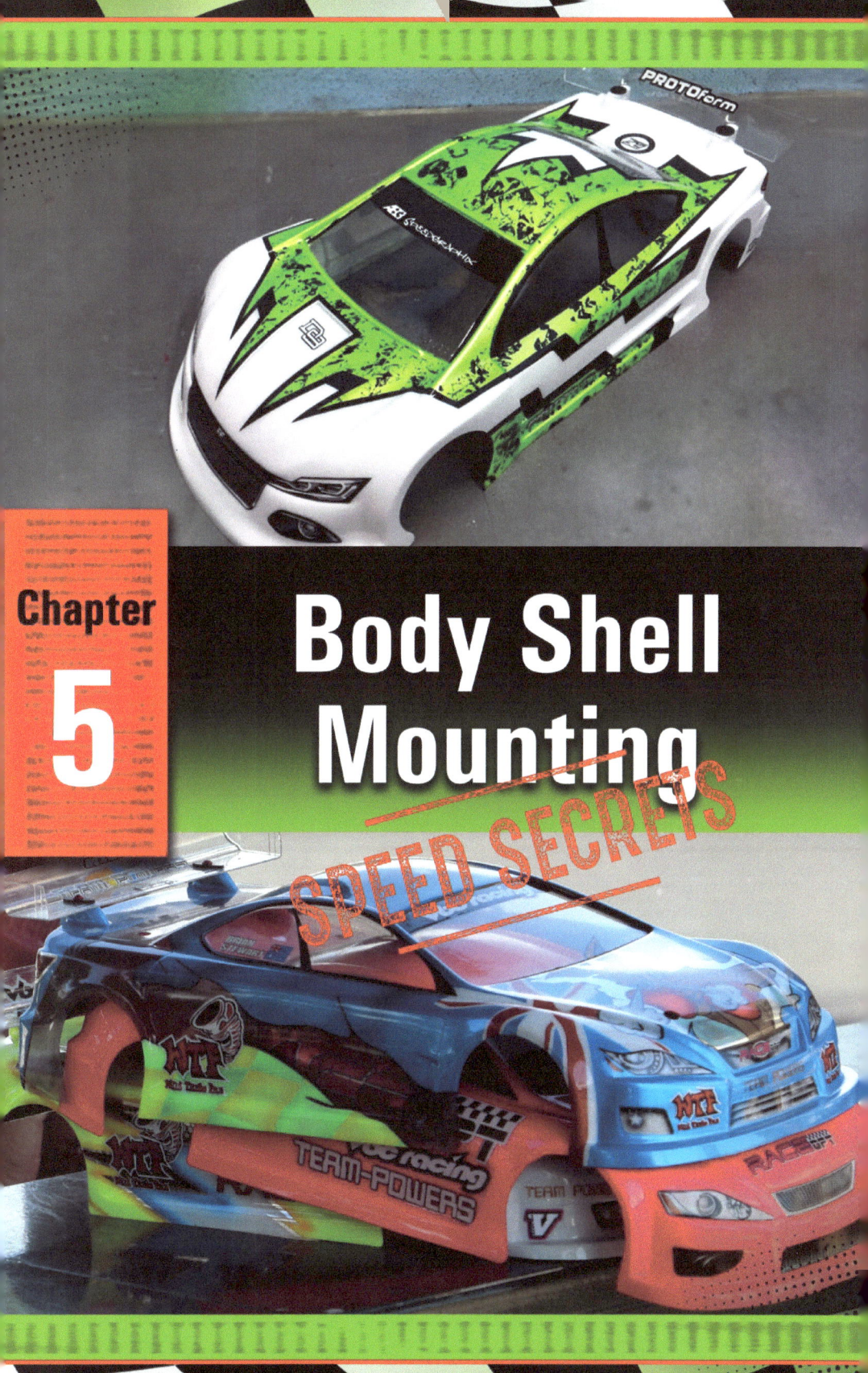

Body Shell Mounting

Chapter 5

SPEED SECRETS

Introduction

Ryan Maker continues his Speed Secrets, taking you through the Body Shell Mounting steps for your car.

Mounting your body shell in the correct position, and preparing it correctly, is critical to a balanced and fast car.

A few years ago, PROTOform and Mon-tech bodies were the stand out in their class and used by 99% of the world's best drivers. However, body shapes are an area that is rapidly evolving, with new bodies being released regularly.

The following are a good place to start currently:

- Xtreme Twister.
- PROTOform Turismo.
- Zoo Racing's latest bodies, including the DBX, Preopard and Baybee.

However, I recommend testing any new body brought out by a reputable manufacturer.

I only ever use light-weight bodies; they are around 15 grams lighter than a regular weight body. The handling difference is quite substantial, and as you can imagine, the lighter body is much more reactive and faster to change direction.

Pro drivers will use bodies made of thinner Lexan. 0.5mm is currently the thinnest available and is what I use. However, 0.7mm is more robust and handles a crash better.

Body Position

Positioning your body in the correct forwards/backwards location is crucial and is a lot easier to achieve when the body shell is clear.

To precisely position the body, a vertical line in the centre of the front wheel arch is required.

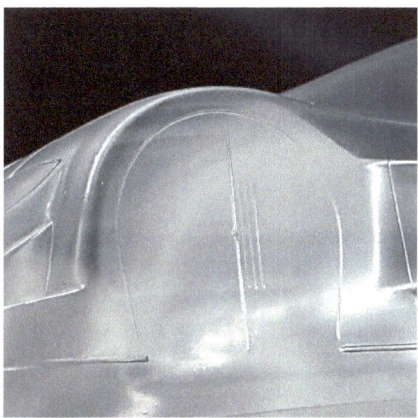 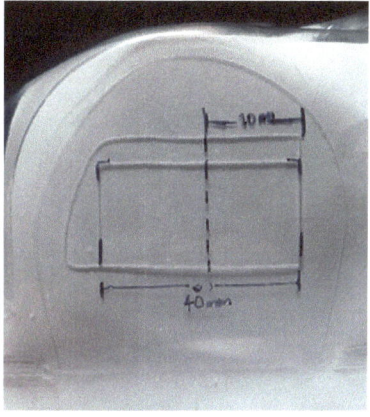

Modern bodies often have this line etched into the body to assist with positioning. In the photo above this PROTOform body has a long vertical line marking the centre of the wheel arch and then three shorter lines towards the rear.

Older PROTOform bodies, have a wing end plate marked in the front wheel arch. You can draw a vertical line in the centre of this rectangle and use this as a reference point in relation to the front axle.

Positioning the axle in front of the vertical line moves the body back, whilst putting the axle behind the line moves the body forward.

As a general rule of thumb I will mount the body 0–6mm forward (axle is behind the line). The further forward the greater the steering provided and the less rear traction. Moving it further forwards than 6mm may adversely affect the car's handling. I don't recommend moving your body rearward (axle in front of the line) as this will only create understeer and slow you down.

Generally, for higher traction tracks when the car has increased stability, you are usually looking for steering, so you would opt for mounting the body further forward. For lower traction tracks you would usually mount the body more around centre or slightly forward, as this creates a nice balance between traction and steering.

When you are marking the body post position on the body, ensure you are locating the body in the middle of the car. You can use the moulding lines on the body as a reference and use callipers from these reference points to your body holes to get it exact. Ream the body post holes so they are slightly bigger than the post. You don't want your body binding on the posts and interfering with the cars flex.

Body Height

Once you have set your desired body position, it's time to cut and set the body height.

Cut your body so that the front lip (splitter) is about 4mm high. Most modern bodies are about right when cut to the mould lines. However, don't make the front splitter less than 2mm high.

If the front splitter is more than 4mm high, then the body will sit too high, raising the centre of gravity too much.

Once you have done this around the entire body, you can set the height of the body on the car. I like to have the front as low as possible, which means if you push the front down under suspension compression, there should be about a 1mm gap between the ground surface and the body. The rear should be adjusted slightly higher than the front; I like to raise the rear of the body slightly to increase the angle (rake). If you push the rear down, there should be about a 2–3mm gap between the bottom of the rear guard and the ground surface.

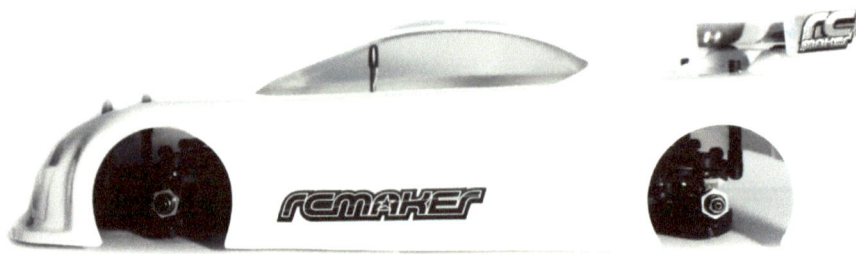

Wheel Arches

Make sure the car is resting at ride height, with the tyres you are using installed and clear body on. Mark the centre of all four axles using a marker pen/sharpie on the outside of the body.

There are several ways to mark the wheel arches. All use curved Lexan body scissors:

1. **Wheel** — Some like to place a wheel/tyre on the body and draw around it as a starting point and adjust from there. This can be hit and miss.

2. **A circle cutter** — I like to use a diameter of 67–68mm, give or take 1mm for different brands of wheels/tyres — you can decide which fits best. Line the pin on the circle cutter up with the centre-rear of the axle for the front, and the bottom rear corner of the axle at the rear. That gives a nicely positioned wheel arch that won't tuck. You can either use it to scribe and then cut with curved scissors, or you can cut the Lexan with the circle cutter to where it's almost cut through all the way, then cut the  very edge with scissors and peel the wheel arch out. The latter isn't for the faint hearted though; the safest is to score and then cut it with scissors.

3. **Template** — Use a dedicated wheel cutter template from RC Maker or MR33. These are designed to make the process simple and accurate:

Once cut out, use your scissors to round the corners of the wheel arches slightly. PROTOform make an amazing sanding drum that works phenomenally for cleaning any imperfections and making a perfectly smooth wheel arch.

Painting

A how-to guide on painting good looking body shells would fill its own book. However, here are some errors to avoid:

- Always start with the darkest colour first.
- Don't use too many thick coats of colour. Thick coats will tend to chip off easily during a crash and add weight to the body.
- Try to keep the total weight of a completed body under 90g (3.17 ounces), including paint and stickers. However, some races have a minimum body weight rule, so check your local regulations.
- Use spray paint designed for Lexan RC body shells. Normal spray paint is not as flexible and will chip off easily in a crash. Your local hobby shop will be able to assist:
    - Tamiya make a range of spray paints. Those with a part number starting with PS are for Lexan RC bodies.
    - If air brushing then Faskolor, PROTOform or Auto-air work well.

If you would like a professionally painted shell then look no further than Nicola670Paint or A83 Speedgraphix. Both have contributed many photos of their work to be showcased in this book (refer to the copyright page of this book to see which photos are theirs):

Nicola670Paint
www.nicola670paint.com

A83 Speedgraphix
@A83 Speedgraphix

Body Shell Mounting 5

A well organised pit space ensures the right tool is at your fingertips

Bumper Foam

I strongly recommend using bumper foam between the body and the bumper, to stop the body folding in at high speed and under hard braking. Depending on how far forward you have mounted your body and your brand of car, you can end up using 0–6mm of bumper foam. Position the foam in the centre of the bumper and stick it to the front of the body on the inside. You can stick foam further out near the corners of the body on the front bumper. However, this is only important on big fast tracks which impose more downforce on your body.

Wing

I mount my wing with a 6mm overhang from the most rear part of the body. Some people like to change its location depending on the track, but I leave it in the same spot all the time. If you move the wing further rearward, you will increase stability or forward provides more steering.

It can be difficult to measure 6mm exactly, so I work off the mounting holes provided by the body manufacturer. If you have a PROTOform body:

- There are 3 pre-marked hole locations on the body. I use the rear-most hole.
- The wing has 2 pre-marked hole locations. I drill a hole exactly halfway between them.

Alternatively, you can use a ruler or square tool (also called a set square) and measure 6mm from the rearmost part of the body. This is where the back of the wing will end. You can now mark the wing hole location with a pen ready for drilling.

I also install the wing endplates, as it finishes the body off and may increase overall stability ever so slightly, especially at high speed. A nice finishing touch to mount your wing are the RC Maker wing washers and wing supports. These support the wing and make installation and removal quick and easy.

Wing Washers   Wing Supports

Chapter 6

Car Setup Reference

Essential Touring Car RC Racer's Guide

This chapter refers to parts of the car as follows:

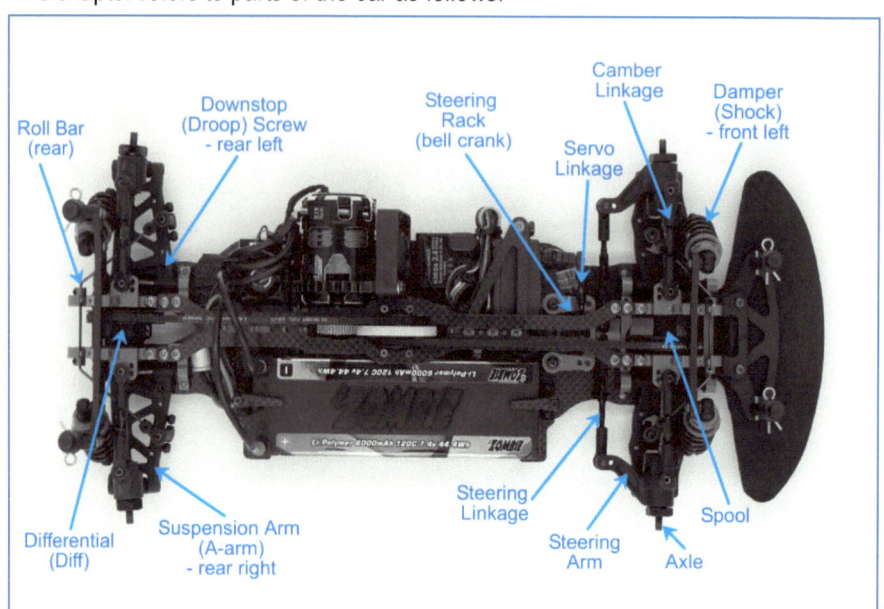

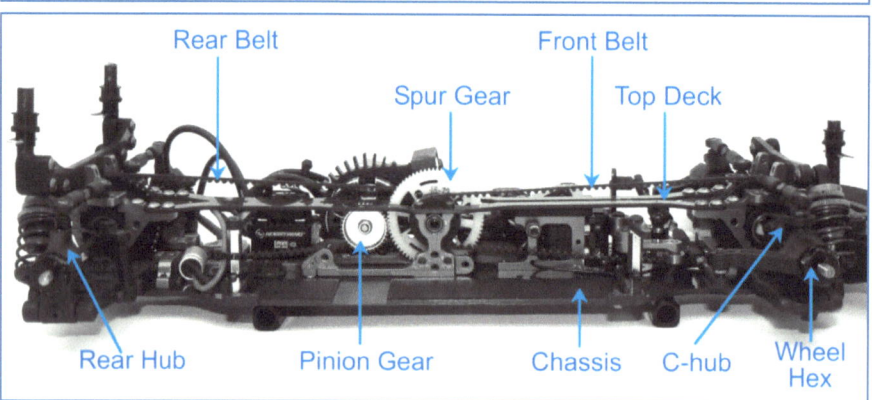

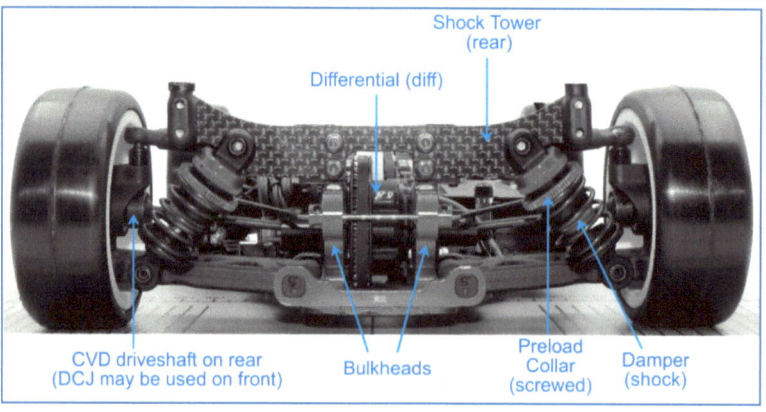

Car Setup Reference 6

In this chapter, we cover the A–Z of setup settings from Ackermann to Wings and everything in between. Where a term used in this chapter is not explained, refer to the *Glossary* on page *215*.

To make the information in this chapter easy to digest, I've given each setup heading a level: Basic, Intermediate or Advanced.

Basic — All racers should be familiar with these headings. They make the largest difference when setting up your car, and I encourage you to develop a thorough understanding of them.

Intermediate — Covers areas that are either more complicated than Basic items, or changing them makes less of a difference to the car's handling. You should aim to develop a good understanding of these areas over time.

Advanced — These headings are the most complex areas. Developing some understanding of these settings over time is beneficial. However, treat them as optional. Many club racers will never change their car's Roll Centre or Ackermann. They are useful fine-tuning tools in order to maximise the car's handling.

Ackermann

Level: Advanced (refer to the previous page for an explanation of levels)

Put simply, the front inside wheel always has a tighter arc in any corner than the front outside wheel. Think of it in terms of the outside of the car having further to go than the inside of the car when turning.

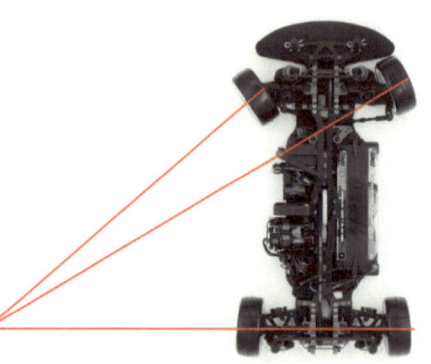

There are many variables which affect the optimum turning angle for the inside and outside tyres (tyre, surface, corner angle, grip, weight, toe, etc). However, let's say that at full lock, with the manufacturer's kit setup, our example car's inside tyre turns 28° (from straight ahead) and the outside tyre only turns 19°. The Ackermann angle is 28–19=9° at full lock. When wheels are straight ahead the Ackermann angle is 0° (assuming no Toe-out is set). The Ackermann angle from 0° (no steering) to 9° (full lock) is not a linear progression, i.e., when half steering lock is applied the angle is unlikely to be 4.5°. The progression depends on the steering linkage angles.

The Ackermann angle is changed by altering the angle of the steering linkages. In the photo below the steering linkages are straight, that is, they are parallel to the axles.

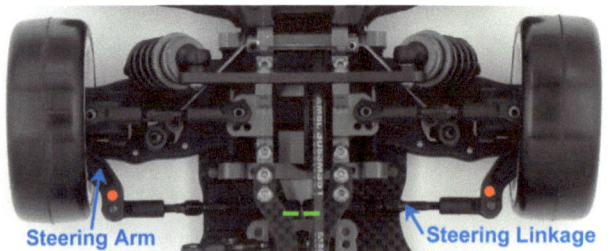

Less Ackermann (for the example car above) — adding shims at the centreline location (green) angles the steering linkages so that at the centreline they are closer to the front of the car (they form a shallow V pointing towards the front of the car). This reduces the Ackermann angle (the difference between how far each tyre turns).

More Ackermann (for the example car above) — using a steering arm hole closer to the front of the car (red) angles the steering linkages so that at the centreline they are closer to the rear of the car (they form a shallow V pointing towards the rear of the car). This increases the Ackermann angle (the difference between how far each tyre turns).

Note: The photo above may not represent your car. Different cars will have different starting angles and different shimming/hole position options. The key to whether you are increasing or reducing Ackermann is the angle of the steering links.

A car's kit setup will usually suggest an Ackermann position where the car is easy to drive, with the best tyre wear (because increasing or decreasing Ackermann from this position increases the slip angle of the tyres).

Setting	By Changing	Handling Impact
Less Ackermann (difference between wheel angles is less)	Steering linkages form a shallow V pointing towards the front of the car.	• Easier to drive. • Car reacts smoothly. • Less initial steering into the corner. • More corner speed. • More traction in the chicane. • Better for smooth flowing tracks with high-speed corners.
More Ackermann (difference between wheel angles is more)	Steering linkages form a shallow V pointing towards the rear of the car.	• Car reacts faster to steering input. • More initial steering into the corner. • Less corner speed. • Less traction in the chicane. • Better for small and tight tracks.

Ackermann is a tuning option used to alter the feeling of the steering curve of the car. More Ackermann refers to more of a difference in angle between the inside and outside tyres. Less Ackermann means the inside and outside tyres are closer together in angle.

Less Ackermann will decrease the difference in angle between the inside and outside tyres, leading to less scrub and less tyre wear. In some conditions, when you have too much aggression, angling the links will help to smooth the car out initially. This setting should give more mid-corner to exit steering, as it maintains more outside steering angle.

> **More Ackermann** will increase the difference in angle between the inside and outside tyres, increasing scrub and tyre wear. This will make the car more aggressive and generally turn harder. However, through mid-corner to exit it may lose steering as the outside wheel doesn't have as much angle.
>
> Generally, a more aggressive Ackermann setting (more Ackermann) is used in low traction to increase the response, and is not used to decrease lap times as much as it is to alter the "feeling" and "balance" of the cars steering characteristics.
>
> — *Ryan Maker*

Ackermann steering geometry changes as the steering input increases. It is a simple concept which can be complex in practice.

Interaction

Front Toe angle (refer page *145*) affects the effectiveness of Ackermann changes. The more front toe-out you have, the greater the Ackermann will be.

Anti-dive (front)

Refer to *Kick-up/Anti-dive* on page *130*.

Car Setup Reference

Anti-squat/Pro-squat (Rear)
Level: Advanced

Anti-squat affects how much the rear of the car "squats down" (settles into the suspension) on-throttle.

The anti-squat angle is often set by spacers under the rear suspension arm mounts. Refer to your car's manual.

No spacers = arms horizontal to chassis = no anti-squat or pro-squat. This is the normal kit setup.

A car with **anti-squat** will have the rear suspension arms tilted "backwards" so that the front of the arm is higher than the rear of the arm. Anti-squat is sometimes referred to as "positive anti-squat".

A car with **pro-squat** will have the rear suspension arms tilted "forwards" so that the front of the arm is lower than the rear of the arm. Pro-squat is sometimes referred to as "negative anti-squat".

Anti-squat	Effect
Anti-squat (front of rear arm is higher than rear of arm)	• Less weight transfer to the rear of the chassis on-power. • Suspension compresses/chassis drops less on-power. • Better on smooth tracks. • Decreases steering response. • Increases rear traction.

Anti-squat	Effect
No anti-squat (rear arms level)	Compared to anti-squat, no anti-squat provides: • More weight transfer to the rear of the chassis on-power. • Suspension compresses/chassis drops more on-power. • Better on bumpy tracks. • Increases steering response.
Pro-squat (front of rear arm is lower than rear of arm)	Not recommended.

Interaction

Re-check your droop after changing Anti-squat.

Arm Sweep

Level: Advanced

Arm sweep is created by using wider suspension block/inserts on the front front, than the front rear suspension block. This angles the arm back (sweep) and will make the car smoother in all parts of the corner and provide slightly more on-power steering. It is good for high traction tracks in order to smooth out an aggressive car, especially on initial turn-in. Negative arm sweep is never used as it has no benefit.

— Ryan Maker

Interaction

Changing the Arm Sweep will change the Toe (refer to page 145).

Battery Position

Level: Intermediate

If your chassis allows the battery to be moved forward or rearward on the chassis then it can be used to tune handling. Shorty lipo batteries may be used for greater flexibility in battery positioning:

Setting	Handling Impact
Forward battery position	• Car is more stable. • Less initial steering. • Less mid-corner rotation. • More steering on-power.
Rearward battery position	• Car is less stable. • More initial steering. • More mid-corner rotation. • Less steering on-power.

This is counter-intuitive. But, adding weight at the rear does not add rear traction, it actually makes it easier for the car to spin out, because of centrifugal force.

For further information refer to page *160*.

Belt Tension

Level: Basic

The more powerful the motor, the tighter the belt tension must be to prevent the belt from skipping during acceleration/deceleration. A skipping belt wastes power and causes the belt to wear. In extreme situations, it could cause the belt to lose teeth and even come off the pulley or diff gear, meaning a DNF.

You should run the belt as loose as possible without the belt skipping. If the belt skips under full power, you should be able to hear it.

A belt that is too tight causes drag on the drivetrain. Low-powered cars, in particular, should run the belt tension as loose as possible.

Refer to your car's manual for instructions on setting the belt tension. It is common for an eccentric diff holder to be used in which case be careful not to change the diff height when setting the belt tension (refer to Diff Height on page *118*).

Higher Powered Cars	Lower Powered Cars
Tighter belt tension	Looser belt tension

Refer to page *54* for further recommendations.

Bodies
Level: Basic

Refer to Body Shell Mounting on page *80*.

Bump Steer
Level: Advanced

When the car goes over a bump, the steering angle may be affected. This is called "bump steer". The car is more susceptible to bump steer when the steering linkage turnbuckle is parallel to the track.

The thickness of the shims under the steering arm ball (shown in green) determines the angle of the steering linkage compared to the chassis.

Steering Linkage Angle	Effect
Smaller angle (closer to parallel to the track)	• Increased in-corner steering. • Car harder to drive. • Better for smooth track. • More susceptible to bump steer.
Greater angle (less parallel to the track)	• Decreased in-corner steering. • Car easier to drive. • Better for bumpy track. • Less susceptible to bump steer.

Bump steer is adjusted through shims under the ball connecting the steering turnbuckle ball cup to the steering arm. It adjusts the amount the wheels toe-in when the suspension compresses. The more shims, the less the toe-out decrease under compression.

Less bump steer shims will make the car smoother, especially on corner entry and is recommended for high traction tracks to smooth the car out.

More bump steer shims will make the car edgier, especially on corner entry, and is generally used on lower traction tracks in order to make the car more aggressive.

— Ryan Maker

Camber

Level: Basic

Camber angle is the angle at which the wheel leans in towards the chassis (negative camber) or away from the chassis (positive camber). In Touring Cars we only use negative camber, as shown in the illustration.

As a general rule, increasing negative camber improves grip on the outside wheel when cornering, thereby increasing steering (within limits, too much negative camber can reduce grip).

Visualise the car as it corners, transferring weight to the tyres on the outside of the corner, i.e., when taking a left-hand corner weight is transferred to the right-hand tyres, and when taking a right-hand corner weight is transferred to the left-hand tyres.

As the weight is transferred to the outside tyres, the car leans towards those tyres. With the correct camber angle, the bottom of the outside front tyre will be flat, or close to it, as the car corners. This maximises the contact patch of the tyre with the racetrack, resulting in the most grip and therefore the most steering.

A rubber tyre tends to roll on itself when cornering. If the tyre had no camber, the inside edge of the tyre would begin to lift from the track, reducing the contact patch. With any negative camber this effect is reduced, thereby maximising the contact patch.

With a 4WD car, there is a compromise between steering and maximising straight-line acceleration, as the greatest traction will be attained when the camber angle is zero, and the tread is flat on the track.

The greater the negative camber angle, the more steering the car has. However, it makes the car more sensitive and harder to drive.

Camber is normally adjusted by shortening or lengthening the upper turnbuckles:

Change	How	Effect
Increase Camber (wheel more angled)	By shortening the turnbuckle	More steering, car more sensitive to steering inputs
Decrease Camber (wheel more upright)	By lengthening the turnbuckle	Less steering, car less sensitive to steering inputs

Initial Camber Setting

Initial Front	Initial Rear
-2 degrees	-2 degrees

You can use this initial setting as your base setup and normally only alter it around 0.5 degrees either side of this. Camber is typically in the range from -1 degrees to -2.5 degrees.

Normally, the left and right tyres at the front will both have the same camber setting, as will the left and right rears.

Check camber frequently:

Fronts — If the front tyre is wearing more on one side, usually the inside, decrease the camber until the tyres wear flat. On rubber tyres this is called a "death ring", on foams it is called "coning".

Rears — Adjust rear camber so that the rear tyres cone slightly to the inside (greater wear on the inside of the tyre).

Interaction

After you set the Camber, re-check the Ride Height and Toe settings. Conversely, after changing the Ride Height re-check the Camber.

The amount of front camber required to maintain the maximum contact patch also depends on the amount of caster. Higher degrees of caster require little or no camber, while lower degrees of caster require more negative camber.

More camber
Increases the car's traction in the middle and exit of the corner, but can cause the car to wear harshly on the inside of the tyre. Adding more camber to one end of the car will cause that end of the car to have more traction in the middle to exit of the corner. Adding more camber to the front will give you better mid-exit steering, while adding more camber to the rear will give you better mid-exit rear stability.

Less camber
Increases the car's traction initially and prevents "death rings". Removing camber from one end of the car will cause that end to have more traction initially, but lose grip through the middle to exit of the corner. Removing camber from the front will make the car turn in hard initially, but have less steering mid-corner and corner exit. It also helps to decrease traction roll problems substantially. Removing camber from the rear will allow it to grip initially when entering a corner, however, throughout the corner as the car rolls, it will lose traction and have decreased stability.

— *Ryan Maker*

Camber Gain

Level: Advanced

Camber gain is how much the camber angle changes as the suspension is compressed. Camber Gain is also referred to as "camber rise" or "camber intake".

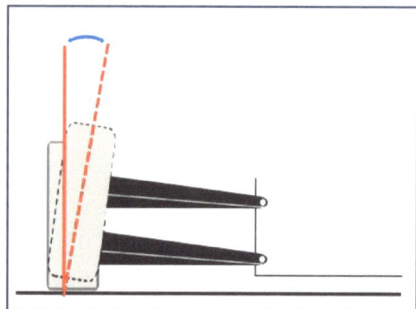

Camber gain is determined by the length of the top and bottom suspension arms (or turnbuckles) and the angle between them. If the top and bottom suspension arms are parallel and the same length, camber will not change as the suspension is compressed. If the angle between the arms is large, or the length of top and bottom arms is different, the camber will increase as the suspension is compressed.

A certain amount of camber gain is desirable to maintain the face of the tyre parallel to the ground as the car rolls into a corner.

Measuring Camber Gain

To measure camber gain, first measure the camber angle (refer to page 98). Next, push on the suspension in the centre of the shock tower, and measure the camber again. The difference between those two camber angles is the camber gain.

Setting Camber Gain

It can usually be adjusted by changing the upper link/arm mount location on the shock tower. However, not all cars offer this adjustment. Refer to your car's manual.

Camber gain occurs when the suspension compresses or rolls. Cars are designed so they feed camber into the tyre as the car rolls, in order to keep the maximum amount of tyre on the ground at all times. Adjusting how much the camber gains/changes can be a very important and useful tuning option, and is tuned via the camber link angle.

More camber gain
Occurs when the upper camber link increases in angle (bulkhead lower relative to hub). You can achieve this two ways, either lowering the link from the inner bulkhead, or raising the link from the outer hub. It is best to work in 0.5mm increments which are noticeable. Increasing the camber gain will increase the car's grip in the middle to exit of the corner, whilst decreasing initial traction. It will also

cause the tyre to wear more aggressively on the inside due to the extra camber gain, so you may experience "death rings". This change can often make the car more aggressive and difficult to drive.

Less camber gain
Occurs when the upper link decreases in angle (bulkhead higher relative to hub). You can achieve this by lowering the outside of the camber link near the hub, or raising the inside on the bulkhead. Decreasing the camber gain will increase the cars initial grip, but decrease traction in the middle and exit of the corner. It will improve the tyre wear in most instances, as the car won't be running as harshly on the inside of the tyre. This is often used to smooth the car out in high traction.

As a general rule of thumb, more camber gain is better for low traction, in order to get the car to generate traction. Less camber gain is better for high traction in order to smooth the car out and make it predictable.

— *Ryan Maker*

Interaction

Higher caster angles will increase camber gain in cornering. Refer to Caster on page *104*.

Camber gain interacts with roll centre to a point, although it may not be noticeable. Refer to Roll Centre on page *141*.

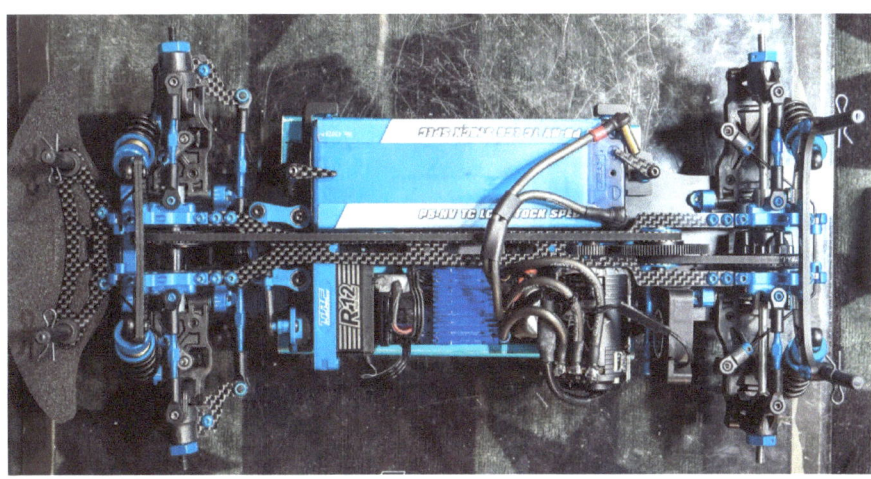

Chassis Stiffness (Flex)

Level: Intermediate

Chassis stiffness is an important factor when setting up your car. Some cars have the option of using a thicker carbon fibre chassis to reduce flex. Others offer an aluminium chassis to virtually eliminate flex.

Typically chassis that provide flex are better for low grip tracks, as they generate more traction and increase in-corner steering, while chassis with less flex are better for high grip surfaces. An aluminium chassis may provide better steering and stability at high grip tracks and are commonly used on carpet.

A stiff chassis also helps eliminate chassis flexing and twisting, which may introduce another factor that is difficult to measure or adjust.

Your car may have set up options which fine-tune the chassis stiffness by changing the mounting of components such as the servo, changing the chassis plate, or other components. Chassis stiffness can therefore be a setup tool and you can make a car "softer" or "stiffer". Refer to your car's manual for options.

There is no right or wrong answer in regard to how much flex a car needs. It is very track dependant, so I would encourage you to test each track to find out what works best there. You can tune it by adding/removing top deck screws and/or motor mount screws. Most manufacturers will instruct you on the flex options of the car in the instruction manual.

More flex is generally better for lower traction tracks, as it makes the car generate more steering and corner speed due to the chassis flexing and making up for any lack of grip generated by the tyres. However, if the car is docile in high traction, it can be useful to liven the car up and make it more responsive. Often adding more flex can work because it masks any problems in the car's geometry or suspension settings. If you are struggling for traction, try removing some top-deck screws. It's surprising how this can sometimes turn an average car into an amazing car.

Less flex is generally better for high traction tracks, as it helps maintain corner speed and stops the car binding up and over gripping in corners. Too much flex can also make the car very twitchy and nosey on high traction tracks, making it very difficult to drive. However, for some low traction tracks, less flex can also work as instead of flexing, the car puts the force back into the suspension and tyres, making them work harder and thus, generating more traction. This is track dependant and should be tested to find the best flex combination. It is a very simple change, so don't be afraid to experiment to find what works best for you, your car and the track.

— *Ryan Maker*

Caster

Level: Advanced

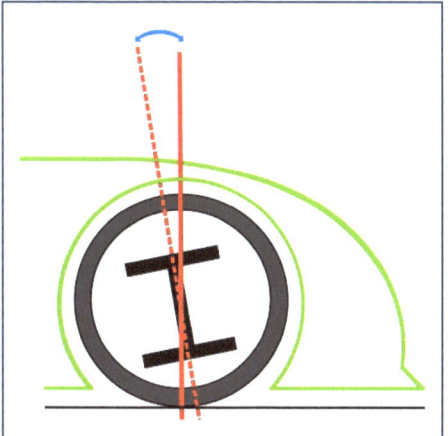
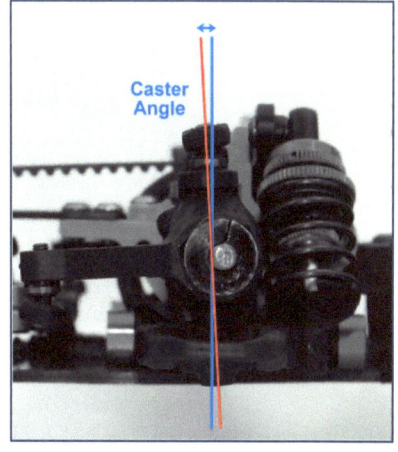

Caster is the angle that the front kingpin leans to the rear of the car from the vertical (vertical being a line perpendicular to the ground). The Caster angle affects on and off-power steering, as it affects the amount the chassis tilts.

Technically, the pivot points of the steering are angled so that a line drawn through them intersects the track surface slightly ahead of the contact point of the tyre. The purpose of this is to provide a degree of self-centring for the steering (the wheel casters around so it trails behind the axis of steering). This makes a car easier to drive and improves its straight-line stability (reducing its tendency to wander). Excessive caster angle will make the steering heavier and less responsive.

Change	Effect
A lesser Caster angle (kingpin more upright)	• Decreases straight-line stability. • Increases off-power steering at corner entry. • Decreases on-power steering at mid-corner and corner exit. • Less stable in bumpy track conditions.
A greater Caster angle (greater kingpin angle from the vertical)	• Increases straight-line stability. • Decreases off-power steering at corner entry. • Increases on-power steering at mid-corner and corner exit. • More stable in bumpy track conditions.

Higher caster angles will increase camber gain in cornering.

Refer to your chassis manufacturer's manual for instructions on changing Caster angle. Typically the caster angle is built into the c-hub and you must change the c-hub to change the caster angle. Make sure you use the same c-hub angle on both sides of the car.

> **More** caster will increase the camber to a **greater** degree as the steering lock is increased, which will provide more high speed and sweeper steering, but less off-power, low-speed steering.
>
> **Less** caster will increase the camber to a **lesser** degree as the steering lock is increased, which will provide more low-speed steering, but less high-speed sweeper steering. This will make the car more aggressive turning into corners.
>
> — *Ryan Maker*

Centre of Gravity

Refer to page 157.

Damping

Level: Intermediate

Damping controls the suspension's travel speed and resistance. An undamped car will oscillate up and down on its springs. With proper damping levels, the car will settle back to a normal state in the minimum time.

Damping	Effect
Softer	• Produces the most grip (both front and rear). • Greater chassis roll. • Decreases cornering speed.
Harder	• Produces the least grip (both front and rear). • Less chassis roll. • Increases cornering speed.

- Damping is controlled by the four shock absorbers.
- The front pair of shock absorbers should always be set the same.
- The rear shock absorbers should always be set the same.
- The front and rear shocks may have different settings.

For tips on building perfect shocks refer to page 56.

Length of Shock

Change	Effect
Longer Shock	**Lengthening** the shock shaft will raise the piston inside the shock body, thus decreasing the volume of oil above the piston and increasing the volume of oil below the piston. • This generates less pack under compression and more under rebound. • Used for high traction tracks. • Less twitchy and easier to drive.
Shorter Shock	**Shortening** the shock shaft will lower the piston inside the shock body, thus increasing the volume of oil above the piston and decreasing the volume of oil below the piston. • This generates more pack under compression and less under rebound. • Used for low traction tracks to generate traction.

This is quite often misunderstood. It does not change droop; it does not change ride height. Actually, what it's changing is where the shock piston sits relative to the shock body. This change can bring on some interesting tuning options.

In **high traction** you generally use a longer shock shaft to decrease the pack and allow the car to collapse into the corner, instead of transferring the pressure to the tyres. Also, the increased shock pack under rebound will slow the weight transfer down on direction change, making the car less twitchy and easier to drive.

In **low traction** you generally use a shorter shock shaft. This increases shock pack under compression, which can give the car the aggression it needs in order to generate traction. Also, having less pack on the rebound stroke allows the car to move around and generate traction.

— Ryan Maker

Oil

The kit oil usually works well in most conditions, but thicker or thinner oil can be used for fine-tuning:

Lower viscosity oil (thinner)	Higher viscosity oil (thicker)
• Faster shock action. • Faster weight transfer. • Suspension works faster and smoothly keeps tyre in contact with track (more traction). • Absorbs the bumps better and therefore better at bumpy tracks. • Takes longer to accelerate out of the corner as the suspension compresses further. • More likely to become unsettled during sharp direction changes (chicanes).	• Slower shock action. • Slower weight transfer. • More stable at high speed and more twitchy at slow speed. • Does not deal with bumps well and therefore better at smooth tracks. • Takes less time to accelerate out of the corner as the suspension compresses less. • Less likely to become unsettled during sharp direction changes (chicanes).

Damping oil and springs work together. If you use thinner oil, consider a softer spring. Similarly, thicker oil works better with a harder spring.

Thinner shock oil (300–400cSt) will make the car softer and more reactive. It will decrease shock pack, which allows the piston to change direction faster and not load up. This generates more traction, but in hot weather can cause the tyres to overheat due to excess chassis roll and movement, making the tyres work overtime. This excess roll and movement also increases the chance of traction roll in high traction.

Thicker shock oil (450–550cSt) will make the car stiffer and less reactive. It will increase shock pack, which causes the piston to lock up more when changing direction. Generates less traction, but will make the car smoother and easier to drive, and look after the tyres in hot weather due to the slowed reaction and less chassis movement. This slower response is generally better for high traction as it makes the car less reactive and less prone to traction rolling.

— Ryan Maker

Piston Holes

The kit number of holes in the shock piston usually works well in most conditions, but changing the number of holes in the piston (or keeping the same number of holes but changing the hole size) can be used for fine-tuning:

Change	Effect
Fewer holes or smaller holes	• Less oil can pass through the piston as it moves. • Provides harder damping — reacts like using thicker oil. • Greater resistance to shock movement and therefore greater damping with slower shock movement.
More holes or larger holes	• More oil can pass through the piston as it moves. • Provides softer damping — reacts like using thinner oil. • Less resistance to shock movement and therefore less damping with faster shock movement.

Less holes (1 or 2) is less common and will increase the shock pack, which causes the piston to lock up when changing direction as there are fewer holes for the oil to travel through. It will make the chassis roll less and roll slower. However, due to the excess shock pack, it can make the car quite twitchy and aggressive initially.

More holes (3 or 4) is a lot more common, especially in big bore shocks where the pistons surface area is increased due to the extra diameter. More holes reduce the shock pack, and can make the car less aggressive around centre, but overall generate more traction. I have found 3 hole to have the best balance, however many drivers using short big bore shocks prefer the 4 hole pistons as they smooth the car out due to the increased size and surface area of the piston.

— Ryan Maker

Position

Different shock position settings change how the shock reacts to compression and how progressive the suspension is.

Change	Front	Rear
More Upright (vertical)	• Less progressive. • Improves on-power steering. • Increases high speed steering.	• Less progressive. • Improves initial acceleration. • Increased rear stability.
More Inclined	• More progressive. • Decreases high speed steering.	• More progressive. • Improves in-corner steering.

Shock Position On Tower

Higher shock position/more vertical (towards the outside of the chassis) will make the shocks harder, increasing initial traction and decreasing chassis roll. One negative regarding higher shock positions is that the shocks can put more pressure on the tyres and make them work harder, thus making them more prone to overheating. In super high traction, it can also generate so much initial traction that it can cause the car to traction roll. This setting is ideal for low traction, where you are trying to generate grip and aggression.

Lower shock position/more inclined (towards the inside of the chassis) will generate less initial traction, increasing initial rotation and providing more traction in the middle and exit of the corner, and more side bite. It increases chassis roll, but decreases the car's willingness to traction roll or overheat tyres, due to the decreased pressure on the tyres. This is more appropriate in high traction to smooth the car out and generate good corner speed.

Staggering shock positions is also common; often I will run the rear shock position higher than the front in order to get more forward traction, especially in low grip. The higher rear shock position will increase initial traction at the rear on-power, and transfer more weight to the tyres, thus increasing the forward traction. However, this will increase steering into the corner as weight transfer to the front will be faster.

— *Ryan Maker*

Shock Position On Arm

Front: Moving the pivot point more inside on the front arm can make the car quite twitchy around centre but understeer overall. Moving the pivot more outside on the front arm will make the car smoother initially, but increase the overall steering. Generally, a position which is furthest out will be the easiest to drive.

Rear: Moving the pivot more inside on the rear arm will increase the car's rotation and provide less on-power rear traction. It can make the car quite "snappy" but may be a good option on smaller tracks if you are suffering from understeer. Moving the pivot more outside will increase overall rear traction and decrease rotation. It makes the car a lot easier to drive and increases the forward traction and stability through corners.

— *Ryan Maker*

Preload

Adjusting preload will change the Ride Height (refer to page 137).

Spring preload is normally set by screwing the collar above the spring so that the spring is more compressed or less compressed. Some cars use preload spacers instead.

Preload	Threaded Collar	Spacers
Increase	**Tighten** collar so it moves down the shock body.	Use **thicker** spacer above the spring.
Decrease	**Loosen** collar so it moves up the shock body.	Use **thinner** spacer above the spring.

Front and rear are adjusted independently. Any preload applied to the left should also be applied to the right.

When using a threaded preload collar, marking the collar with a pen can make it easier to make the same change left-to-right. You can also measure the gap from the bottom of the shock cap to the top of the preload collar and ensure it is the same left-to-right.

Compressing the spring using the preload collar does not change the force applied by the spring. However, if you compress the spring further than the natural weight of the car does, you are reducing the travel of the shock (and therefore the travel of the suspension).

Rebound

Remove the damper spring and push the shock shaft all the way into the shock body. When you let it go, the amount the shock shaft rebounds out of the shock body is the amount of rebound. If it doesn't move at all, then rebound is 0%, if it comes out half way it's 50% and if it rebounds fully, then it's 100%. Rebound may be any percentage from 0–100%.

Rebound can fine-tune the feel of the car. Some pro drivers prefer less rebound or even 0% rebound.

Change	Feel of the Car
More Rebound (higher %)	• Makes the car feel more responsive. • Car will be "bouncier" over bumps.
Less Rebound (lower %)	• Makes the car feel less responsive. • Car will be less "bouncy" over bumps and therefore easier to drive on a bumpy track.

More rebound will generate more traction, as it is constantly trying to force the tyre back onto the ground, like an extra spring. This makes the car more agile, increasing chassis movement. Normally in low grip you will use more rebound to increase the car's aggression and ability to generate traction. I recommend never using more than 50% rebound, as it can make the car snappy and aggressive.

Less rebound will generate less traction, as there is no force pushing the tyre back to the ground. This makes the car smoother and decreases chassis movement.

> This normally works best in high traction when the car is already moving around due to the extra grip. Generally, you will decrease your rebound in high traction in order to decrease the chance of traction roll and make the car easier to drive.
>
> — *Ryan Maker*

To Set Rebound

1. Assemble the shock as per the manufacturer's instructions. This will normally provide 100% rebound.
2. Release the shock cap by 2–3 turns.
3. Push the shock shaft fully into the shock body. Depending on the design of the shock, oil will probably release through the overflow hole in the shock cap.
4. Tighten the shock cap. Oil will normally release through the overflow hole in the cap.
5. Test Rebound.
6. Repeat steps 2–5 until you obtain the rebound % you prefer.

Springs

The springs determine the amount of chassis roll, and how quickly the chassis rolls.

If the car is rolling significantly, it will create a great deal of grip due to more weight being transferred onto the outside tyres in the turn. This is good for low grip tracks. But on high grip tracks, this will decrease the corner speed and slow the "change of direction" responsiveness.

When do you know whether you have the best spring tension combination? Refer to the table below:

	Springs Too Soft	"Best" Spring Rate	Springs Too Hard/Stiff
Low Grip Track	This situation is the hardest to identify. Car will be slower in the corners than it could be.	Springs soft enough to generate sufficient grip without unduly slowing the car.	Car will grip initially, but part way into a corner, well before the apex, the rear end will break away suddenly and substantially.
High Grip Track	Decreases the corner speed and slows the 'change of direction' responsiveness.	Harder springs while still generating sufficient grip without unduly slowing the car.	Car 'hops' or 'chatters' across the track when cornering.

In order to minimise lap times, aim to limit the chassis roll as much as possible by using harder springs without the car chattering or the rear end breaking away unexpectedly. Of course, you still need sufficient rear grip to accelerate as early as possible out of the corners, and sufficient front grip to generate the steering you want. As with all car setup, it is about finding the best balance for your driving style at the current track.

The kit spring usually works well in most conditions, but a harder or softer spring can be used for fine-tuning:

Stiffness	Front	Rear
Softer spring	• More overall grip. • Decreased steering response. • Smoother steering. • Increased off-power steering. • Increased mid-corner steering. • Smoother under braking.	• More overall grip. • Increased in-corner steering. • Increased on-power steering. • Decreased mid-corner steering.
Harder spring	• Less overall grip. • Increased steering response. • Increased in-corner steering. • Increased on-power steering. • Decreased mid-corner steering.	• Less overall grip. • Increased mid-corner steering. • Improved initial acceleration.

The tension of the front springs and the tension of the rear springs are often different. However, the spring tension on the left and right must be the same.

Damping oil and springs work together. If you use thinner oil, consider a softer spring. Similarly, thicker oil works better with a harder spring.

Differential

Level: Basic

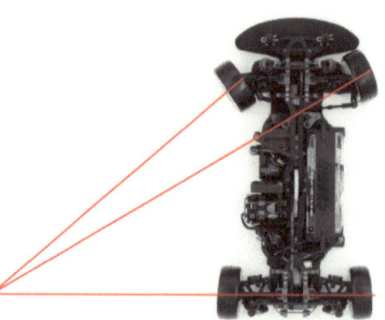

The wheel on the outside of a turn always has to travel farther than the inside wheel. The front wheels turn at different angles to allow for this (refer to Ackermann on page *90*). The rear wheels use a differential, or diff, to allow the wheels to turn at different speeds and this assists the car to rotate into corners.

Gear diffs have largely replaced ball diffs due to their consistency and lack of maintenance.

Gear Diff

Most modern kits come with a gear differential. They are also available from third-party suppliers. They increase on-power steering compared to ball diffs.

Gear diffs require significantly less maintenance than ball diffs, but use oil viscosity for adjustments rather than a simple nut. Modified cars tend to use thicker oil. The manufacturer should provide a recommended starting point for oil viscosity.

Low Traction	Medium Traction	High Traction	Very High Traction
1,000–2,000 cSt	2,000–5,000 cSt	5,000–10,000 cSt	10,000–20,000 cSt

As a general rule, thinner oil increases traction and thicker oil increases on-power steering and stability.

Setting	Rear Diff
Higher viscosity oil (thicker)	• Less traction. Used for higher traction conditions. • Better acceleration. • Less stability. • More on-power steering. • Harder for the car to rotate into the corner. • Less off-power steering.
Lower viscosity oil (thinner)	• More traction. Used for lower traction conditions. • Less acceleration. • Greater stability. • Less on-power steering. • Easier for the car to rotate into the corner. • More off-power steering.

A diff is always used at the rear. Some drivers use a diff at the front of the car as well. However, it is more common to use a solid axle in the front (refer to page *143*). A diff in the front increases on-power steering and cornering speed.

Setting	Front Diff
Higher viscosity oil (thicker)	• Smoother steering response. • More forward traction. • More on-power steering. • Less off-power steering. • Better stability when braking. • Lower cornering speed.
Lower viscosity oil (thinner)	• More aggressive steering response. • Less forward traction. • Less on-power steering. • More off-power steering. • Less stability when braking. • Higher cornering speed.

Front diffs tend to benefit from thicker oils. The thicker the oil the closer the driving feel is to that of a solid axle. Solid axles are lighter than diffs.

Refer to page *53* for tips on building your gear diff.

Ball Diff

Setting	Handling Impact
Tighter diff	Better acceleration, harder for the car to rotate into the corner.
Looser diff	Less acceleration, easier for the car to rotate into the corner.

How Tight Should the Diff Be?

I tighten the diff with a wrench so it is tight (without cranking down), then let off 1/4 of a turn. For a tighter diff let off less than a quarter turn, for a looser diff let off more than a quarter turn. A tight diff may turn the motor over when you check the diff action.

Check the Diff Action

Put the car on the stand and turn the right wheel clockwise. The left wheel should turn anti-clockwise. If it doesn't, then check you have assembled your diff as per the manufacturer's instructions. The diff should feel reasonably smooth. It is unnecessary for the diff to be perfectly smooth with no gritty feel at all, but the smoother the diff feels, the better it will perform.

Running in the Diff

After re-building the diff, and before checking the diff tightness, run the diff in by holding one of the rear wheels and providing a little throttle to spin the other wheel. Don't run at full throttle and don't run for more than a couple of seconds. Then hold the other wheel and do the same thing.

Checking the Diff Tightness

Hold the right wheel and diff with your right hand and use your left hand to try and turn the left wheel. The left wheel should be very difficult to rotate. If it is not, then tighten or loosen the diff nut slightly and re-test until the desired result is achieved.

The "Diffing Out" Problem

Put your car on a stand so that all the wheels are off the ground. Hold one of the rear wheels and apply some throttle.

You should notice that the wheel you aren't holding will spin twice as fast as it normally would for that amount of throttle.

Imagine that the wheel you are holding is the wheel on the outside of the corner and your car is leaning on this wheel. This outside wheel has most of the weight of the car, giving it more traction, and the inside wheel will have less weight on it and therefore less traction, allowing it to possibly break traction and start spinning. This is a "diff out" and will cause your back end to oversteer.

A tighter ball diff will assist to prevent "diffing out" (for a gear diff try a thicker diff oil).

Ball Diff Rebuild

The ball diff should be rebuilt periodically, typically when it feels "gritty" when rotating one rear tyre by hand, or if it is no longer smooth, indicating it may need re-greasing.

Rebuild by disassembling and thoroughly cleaning the various parts of the diff. Check the diff rings. If they have a line scored into them by the diff balls then replace, or remove the line by sanding the diff rings using 600 grit wet and dry sandpaper. Wet the sandpaper with brake cleaner and sand the rings in circles until the groove is removed. Clean rings with brake cleaner and a rag after sanding.

Diff Height

Diff height is an adjustment that can be made on most top-level touring cars via the eccentric diff/spool holder and adjusts the driveshaft angle into the outdrives. Depending on the manufacturer, this setting may also adjust belt tension (refer to page 96).

Setting	Front Diff/Spool	Rear Diff
Upper Position (High Diff)	• Less front traction. • More steering. • Use for medium-high traction tracks/technical tracks.	• Less rear traction. • More on-power steering. • Use for medium-high traction tracks.
Lower Position (Low Diff)	• More front traction. • Pushes on-power. • Use for low traction tracks.	• More rear traction (mainly on-power). • More stable in chicane. • Pushes on-power. • Use for low-medium traction tracks.

> **High** diffs will smooth the car out and make it easier to drive as there is less 'binding' in the drive shafts. This is often better for higher traction tracks to help the car maintain corner speed and make it easier to drive.
>
> **Low** diffs will make the car more aggressive and generate more initial traction as there is more 'binding' in the drive shafts. This is often better for low traction tracks in order to generate grip and aggression.
>
> — *Ryan Maker*

Droop

Level: Basic

Droop is the amount of suspension travel the car has (and is normally different at the front and rear of the car).

With the body off, place your car on the floor so that the tyres just touch the ground and no more. Now let go of the car and watch the chassis lower as the suspension settles. This down travel as the suspension settles is droop. Take hold of the car with one hand on each shock tower and slowly lift until the wheels just start to come off the ground. This up travel is also droop.

Droop is an important tuning option as it is the amount of suspension travel the car has available to transfer weight when the car accelerates or brakes.

Measuring Droop

The easiest way to quickly measure droop is with two 10mm thick droop blocks to rest the chassis on and a droop gauge.

1. Remove the tyres. Shocks and roll bars should be attached.

2. Place the chassis on droop blocks on a flat surface. The chassis should be parallel to the table.

Droop Blocks

3. Check that the suspension is settled by tapping the camber link of the suspension arm that you're checking.

4. Place the droop gauge under the suspension arm. Where the arm touches the gauge is the current droop. **NB:** if the bottom of the arm has screws or protrusions, then ignore these and try to measure at the bottom of the arm. Always measure in the same place.

Car Setup Reference

Straight Droop Gauge

Circular Droop Gauge (from MR33)

5. Repeat step 4 on the other side of the car.
6. Repeat steps 3–5 for the other end of the car.

Alternatively, if you don't have a droop gauge, you can use a ruler as follows:

1. Put the tyres on the car. Car should be race ready.
2. Place the car on a flat surface, on its wheels.
3. Push down and release the front and rear of the car so that the suspension settles.
4. Use a ruler to measure the **starting ride height** at the bottom of the chassis in the centre (front or rear).

5. Leave the ruler in place and lift the car by the centre of the shock tower (the front shock tower if measuring front droop or the rear tower for rear droop) until the wheels just leave the ground. Now measure the **ending ride height**. The difference in the starting and ending ride heights is the droop.

6. Repeat steps 3–5 for the other end of the car.

NB: Using a ruler is less accurate and less repeatable than using a droop gauge. It requires a steady hand. It also requires that you judge the moment the tyres leave the ground (and of course the rubber tyres make this judgement difficult as the tyres will have some sag). A droop measurement taken with a gauge will be different to one taken with a ruler.

It doesn't matter whether you use a gauge or a ruler as long as you are consistent. If discussing Droop with another racer, make sure you know which they are talking about.

Adjusting Droop

- Droop is adjusted using the downstop screws (often referred to as droop screws). There is a downstop screw for each suspension arm.
- Downstop screws limit how far the suspension arm travels downward (which determines how far upwards the chassis can travel).
- If the downstop screw is not touching the chassis, then it is not having any effect.
- Left droop must equal right droop.
- Front droop and rear droop are set independently.

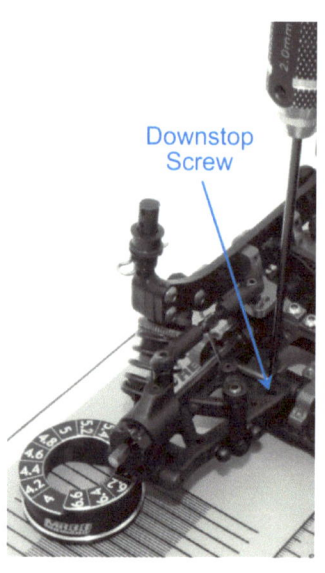

Downstop Screw

Setting	Droop Gauge	Downstop Screw
More Droop	Lower Number	Screw out the downstop screw so that the lower arm drops slightly.
Less Droop	Higher Number	Screw in the downstop screw so that the lower arm rises slightly.

Rear Droop

Starting Rear Droop: Refer to your car manual for your manufacturer's starting droop recommendation. Droop is not always comparable between car brands due to the different thickness of the suspension arms and similar factors. If your manufacturer does not specify a starting droop setting, then use 6mm on the gauge.

Setting	Handling Impact
Increase Droop	• Increases rear chassis upward travel off-power and under braking. • Increases forward weight transfer. • More steering. • Less stable and harder to drive. • Better on bumpy tracks.
Decrease Droop	• Decreases rear chassis upward travel off-throttle and under braking. • Decreases forward weight transfer. • More stable under braking. • More stable on-power. • Better on smooth tracks. • More rear traction.

Increasing rear droop (lower number) will increase the weight transfer to the front, especially off-power. This will give the car more steering and rotation off-power and on-power. It gives the car more overall steering and generally makes it harder to drive. Usually you will add rear droop when looking for more steering and rotation. Too much rear droop on low traction can make the car very difficult to drive.

Decreasing rear droop (higher number) will decrease the weight transfer to the front, especially off-power. This will give the car more stability off-power, and more on-power stability. It gives the car more overall rear traction and makes it easier to drive. Not enough rear droop can make the car "bind up" in the corner and lead it to lack rotation and steering.

— Ryan Maker

Front Droop

Starting Front Droop: Refer to your car manual for your manufacturer's starting droop recommendation. Droop is not always comparable between car brands due to the different thickness of the suspension arms and similar factors. If your manufacturer does not specify a starting droop setting then use 5mm on the gauge.

Setting	Handling Impact
Increase Droop	• Increases upward chassis travel on-power. • Increases rearward weight transfer. • More responsive, less stable. • Better on bumpy tracks. • More rear traction.
Decrease Droop	• Decreases front chassis upward travel on-power. • Less rearward weight transfer. • Less responsive, more stable. • Better on smooth tracks.

Front droop is a good tuning option to adjust the aggressiveness of the car. If the car is too aggressive, add front droop. If it is not aggressive enough, remove front droop.

Increasing front droop (lower number) will increase weight transfer to the rear, especially on-power. This can increase rear traction on-power and increase high-speed steering, due to centrifugal forces acting on the rear of the car while it is loaded up. It will, however, decrease initial turn-in and low-speed steering.

Decreasing front droop (higher number) will increase initial turn-in and slow speed steering. It decreases rear stability on-power and makes the car more stable at high speed.

— Ryan Maker

Interaction

Changing the droop will change the ride height. Refer to Ride Height Interactions on page *138*. Always check the ride height after changing the droop, and vice versa.

Increasing the ride height will decrease the droop value. Decreasing the ride height will increase the droop value.

Changing tyre brands may change the ride height, and therefore the droop.

ESC Settings

Level: Basic

Blinky (non-timing mode) — Stock classes normally require the ESC to be in "Blinky" mode. "Blinky" denotes a mode of the ESC with no dynamic timing. This is often shown by a blinking light on the ESC — hence "Blinky". It is also referred to as "non-timing mode". There are no such restrictions for the Modified class.

Brake Strength — Set brake strength to 100% and then reduce the brake EPA on the radio until you are comfortable with the brake force.

Drag Brake — Drag brake is the amount of brakes applied when the throttle is in neutral. Some drivers swear by it, while others prefer not to use it. It can be a useful tuning aid and changes the feel of the car when entering a corner.

Reverse is illegal for racing, so disable it.

Throttle — In Stock classes this will normally be set to maximum. In Modified, set the aggressiveness of the throttle on the ESC to a medium or midway setting initially and tune from there.

Turbo & Boost — You can set your ESC to advance the motor timing electronically to provide higher top end RPM using the turbo and boost settings. Refer to your ESC manual for instructions. Turbo and boost are not usually legal in Stock classes, refer to your local rules. For examples of this setting refer to the Case Studies chapter on page 172.

> Some ESCs will look for Wide Open Throttle (WOT) for a period of time in order to engage turbo (i.e., advance the motor timing). Your radio might send a signal of -100 for full brake, 0 for neutral, and 100 for full throttle (WOT). Radios send the throttle signal to the receiver in the car many times per second. If you have pulled full throttle and not changed your finger on the trigger then the radio should send 100, 100, 100, 100, etc until you take your finger off full throttle. Unfortunately, some radios may "wander" and might send 100, 100, 99, 100, 100, 101, 100, 98, etc. Therefore the ESC might not see WOT for the period it needs to engage turbo because when it sees a value less than 100 (in our example) it thinks you've reduced throttle on purpose.
>
> To fix this, go into the settings on your radio and choose End Point Adjustment (or EPA). There is normally an EPA setting for both Steering

124

and Throttle. Change your Throttle EPA setting to 110%. Now when you squeeze full throttle, your radio will send 110, 110, 109, 110, 110, 111, 110, 108 (in our example). Therefore the ESC will see a number greater than 100 and knows you are at WOT and the turbo will kick in after the time specified in the settings.

Note: if you must re-synchronise your radio with your ESC then set the throttle EPA back to 100% before doing so. Once re-synchronised change it back to 110%.

Flex

Refer to Chassis Stiffness (Flex) on page *103*.

Gearing & Rollout

Level: Basic

The correct gearing is essential to minimise your lap times. Gearing determines both acceleration and top speed.

The "best" gearing for you depends on your driving style, the track environment, and the motor/chassis setup. It is therefore likely that you will change your gearing for different tracks. A large flowing track might benefit from higher top speed, while a smaller and tighter track might benefit from better acceleration out of the corners.

Gearing for Final Drive Ratio or Rollout?

Touring cars have a Final Drive Ratio (FDR) often called "gear ratio" or "ratio" or "gearing". FDR is the number of times the motor must turn so that the wheels turn once. Expressed as a ratio, e.g., 4.0:1 means the motor turns four times to rotate the wheels once.

However, if you use foam tyres then you most likely use Rollout rather than FDR. Rollout is how far the car will move forward with one revolution of the motor. This depends on your FDR and the diameter of the tyres. As tyre diameter reduces, the work the motor does changes. TQ RC Racing has an excellent Rollout Calculator (www.tqrcracing.com).

Tyres	Wear	FDR or Rollout
Rubber	Minimal	FDR
Foam	Significant reduction of tyre diameter (by mm per race meeting)	Rollout

Final Drive Ratios

Lower FDR's provide higher RPM and therefore faster top speed, but less torque and therefore slower acceleration. Lower means "less than" so 3.0:1 is lower than 4.0:1.

Higher FDR's provide lower RPM and therefore slower top speed, but more torque and therefore greater acceleration. Higher means "greater than" so 4.0:1 is higher than 3.0:1.

Calculating the Final Drive Ratio (FDR)
FDR = (Spur / Pinion) x Internal Ratio

The internal ratio will be specified in your car's manual.

For example, an 80 tooth spur gear with a 35 tooth pinion and an internal ratio of 1.8 provides an FDR of 80/36 x 1.8 = 3.996 (and I'll round this to 4). This means 4:1, or the motor turns 4 times for every 1 time that the wheels turn.

Gear Ratio Charts

It can be handy to make your own gear ratio charts to refer to. There are many websites that will create a chart based on a range of spur and pinions you specify. For example: Gear Machine (www.gearmachine.net).

So What FDR Should You Start With?

Where your motor's manufacturer does not provide recommended starting gearing, you can use the following table as a starting point. Always check the temperature carefully when gearing a new motor for the first time (refer to Motor Temperature on page 129).

Brushless Motor	Starting FDR (Medium Sized Track)
3.5 turns	8.6:1
4.5 turns	7.8:1
5.5 turns	7.2:1
6.5 turns	6.8:1
8.5 turns	6.2:1
10.5 turns	5.5:1
13.5 turns	4.5:1
17.5 turns	4.0:1
21.5 turns	3.7:1
25.5 turns	3.5:1

NB: for foam tyres refer to Rollout below.

Many racers will use a lower FDR than shown above. However, the above is a good starting point.

Things you should consider when setting your FDR:

- All motors are not created equally. Always follow the motor manufacturer's gearing recommendation.
- Track (open with long straight = lower, or short and tight = higher).

- Whether you have advanced the end bell motor timing (see below).
- Air temperature (see Motor Temperature below).

What Rollout Should You Start With?

Rollout is how far the car will move forward with one revolution of the motor.

Rollout is more often used with foam tyres as it takes into account tyre wear to provide accurate gearing. Change the pinion gear as necessary to maintain the same Rollout. However, foam tyres are rarely run on electric touring cars.

Calculating the Rollout

(Tyre Diameter x 3.14) / ((spur gear / pinion gear) x internal ratio)

For example, a car with 64mm diameter tyres with an 80 tooth spur gear, 35 tooth pinion and an internal ratio of 1.8 provides:

> (64mm x 3.14) / ((80 / 35) x 1.8) = a 50.29mm rollout. I.e., the car will move forward approximately 50mm every time the motor rotates once.

Gear Mesh

Setting the correct gap between the pinion gear and the spur gear is vital. If the gap is too large, the spur gear will strip, if the gap is too small the spur will cause drag on the pinion (often accompanied by excessive gear noise and motor overheating). Some sources suggest 0.3mm of play between the spur and pinion gear teeth. However, this is difficult to measure. If you shine a torch on the mesh, you should see a very small gap. Another option is to run a small piece of paper between the gears by turning the spur gear. It should feed all the way through and drop out. If it won't, then the mesh is too tight. Lastly, you can hold the pinion and rock the spur back and forth; there should be a little play. Modified mesh has slightly less play than Stock to prevent stripping the spur gear with the greater torque. For photo examples refer to page 243.

End Bell Timing

You can increase the RPM of a brushless motor by advancing the motor timing. This is often done by loosening the end bell screws and rotating the end bell. You can see in the photo that the example motor is set to 45 degrees of end bell timing. To increase RPM, increase the timing, e.g., to 50 degrees. Some notes of caution:

1. Increasing the end bell timing will increase your motor temperature (see Motor Temperature below).
2. Increasing end bell timing will reduce motor torque, i.e., the motor will have a faster top speed (RPM) but will accelerate slower (torque).
3. Never increase motor timing past the last timing mark by the manufacturer.
4. To increase motor timing, loosen (but don't remove) the screws and rotate the end bell. Most motors use a similar system for changing timing.

Tuning Gearing for the Lowest Lap Times

Electric motors generate maximum torque at 1 RPM and the torque declines as the RPM increases. It is possible to lose too much low-end torque to effectively accelerate the weight of the car from a slow corner.

Track	Gearing	Result
Small, tight track	Smaller pinion	More torque, less top end RPM
Large, open track	Larger pinion	Less torque, higher top end RPM

Caution: changing gearing may affect Motor Temperature (see below).

Selecting the "best" gearing for a particular track is a compromise and often involves trial and error by changing the gearing and watching the lap times to see if they are faster or slower.

To speed up this process when you race at a new track, ask other drivers that are using the same brand and model of motor for their FDR/Rollout recommendation.

Motor Temperature

Take the temperature of the motor using an infra-red temperature gauge. Some motors are more susceptible to heat than others, but as a rule of thumb, we want to make sure that our motor is 72°C (162°F) or less at the end of a race. If it is between 72°C and 80° C (176°F), then decrease the size of the pinion by 1 tooth or decrease the end bell timing by a couple of degrees. The motor can handle 80°C occasionally, but the motor life will not be as long as motors that operate at 72°C. If it is over 80°C then, unfortunately, the motor may have been damaged.

If it is under 65°C (149°F) at the end of the race, then you can risk lowering the FDR by increasing the size of the pinion by 1 tooth, or increasing the end bell timing by a couple of degrees.

Wait until your motor has cooled down and drive some more laps, this time stopping every 1 minute and taking the temperature.

Repeat the process until the car is as fast as you can make it while coming off the track at 72°C (162°F) or less.

If on race day the air temperature is hotter than when you carried out your testing, then consider raising the FDR or lowering the end bell timing so you don't overheat the motor.

Overheating melts the solder inside the motor, and soon afterwards the motor will probably stop working. It might just go slowly, or it might grind to a halt in the middle of a race and start smoking! Motors that have overheated tend to smell (forever).

Tip: A fan and/or motor heat sink will assist to dissipate heat.

Kick-up/Anti-dive (Front)
Level: Advanced

Kick-up affects how much the front of the car dives down (settles into the suspension) off-throttle and under braking.

The kick-up is set by spacers under the front suspension arm mounts or via inserts for the hinge pin. Refer to your car's manual.

No spacers = arms horizontal to chassis = no kick-up or anti-dive. This is the normal kit setup.

A car with **kick-up** will have the front suspension arms tilted "backwards" so that the front of the arm is higher than the rear of the arm. Kick-up is sometimes referred to as "negative anti-dive".

A car with **anti-dive** will have the front suspension arms tilted "forwards" so that the front of the arm is lower than the rear of the arm. Anti-dive is sometimes referred to as "positive anti-dive".

Kick-Up	Effect
Kick-Up (front of front arm is higher than rear of arm)	• More weight transfer to the front of the chassis off-power and under braking. • Suspension compresses/chassis drops more off-power and under braking. • Better on bumpy tracks. • Decreases steering response.
No Kick-up or Anti-dive (front arms level)	Kit setup.
Anti-dive (front of front arm is lower than rear of arm)	• Less weight transfer to the front of the chassis off-power and under braking. • Suspension compresses/chassis drops less off-power and under braking. • Better on smooth tracks. • Increases steering response.

Interaction

Adding kick-up increases Caster (refer page *104*). Adding anti-dive will reduce Caster.

Also re-check your droop after changing kick-up/anti-dive.

Motor Mount Location

Level: Basic

Until 2019 rear mounted motors were standard:

Rear-motor Mount (ESC in front of motor)

However, mid-mount motors have increased in popularity. Many modern kits offer a mid-mounted motor where the motor is mounted further forward than the historical rear mounted motor. For ease of description these are referred to as mid-mounts, although details vary by manufacturer, including:

- The spur gear might be in front of, or behind, the motor.
- Front and rear belts might be equal length, or one might be slightly longer than the other.

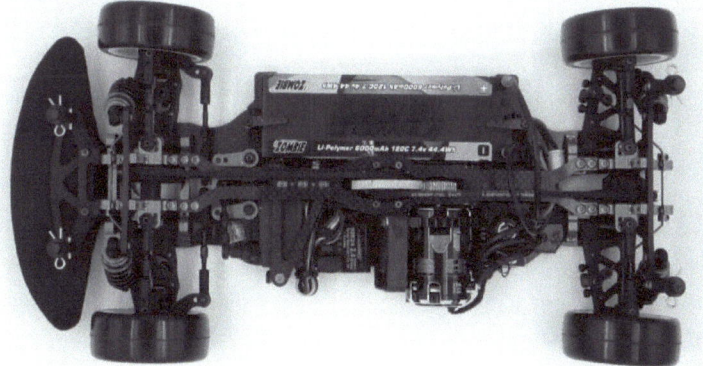

Mid-motor Mount (ESC behind motor)

Some manufacturers offer the choice of rear mount or mid-mount version, and some offer both options with the kit.

Third-party manufacturers offer conversion kits from rear mount to mid-mount.

A mid-mount car may be easier to drive than one with a rear mount. When the heavy, rigid motor is mounted close to the middle of the chassis, the car is more predictable and the rear has greater flex, improving grip. Some manufacturers provide rear stiffeners which can be used to tune this additional flex.

The equal, or close to equal, belt lengths of mid-mount cars delivers power more evenly.

Pro-squat

Refer to Anti-squat/Pro-squat (Rear) on page 94.

Radio Settings

Level: Basic

The following are general guidelines for use as a starting point.

Too Much Steering

If your car has a lot of steering, you can change radio settings to reduce it. This might be useful when you have limited practice time (such as at an event) and there is insufficient time to return to the pits and change the setup:

- **Steering Curve (Expo)** — If the slightest input gives a lot of steering you can slow this down by using negative steering expo. -15% to -20% is a good starting point which will soften the initial steering input and allow the car to react gradually, without changing the total steering available.

- **Dual Rate** — refer to page 75.

- **End Point Adjustment (EPA) Servo setting** — reducing the EPA to less than 100% will reduce the amount of steering. However, it is recommended that you use Expo or Dual Rate rather than EPA to reduce steering. If you change the EPA then make the same change for left and right so that turning to the left and right remains equal. Refer to steering throw on page 144.

Too Much Power for the Conditions

Throttle Expo — You can use negative expo to mellow out the throttle input if there is low traction.

Ride Height

Level: Basic

Overview

Ride height is measured with the wheels on the car and the car ready-to-race except for the body. Ride height affects the car's traction (as it alters the centre of gravity and roll centre).

Setting	Effect
Decreasing Ride Height (lowering the car)	• Smoother steering response. • Reduces chassis roll. • Increases cornering grip but decreases forward traction. • Better on smoother tracks and on these may corner faster. • Reduces likelihood of traction rolling.
Increasing Ride Height (raising the car)	• Steering response more reactive. • Increases chassis roll. • Increases overall grip. • Better on bumpy and asphalt tracks. • Increases likelihood of traction rolling.

Ride height can be altered to change the balance of the car and its ability to absorb bumps.

Increasing ride height
Increasing the front and rear ride height will make the car more stable, and increase its ability to handle bumps. However, on high traction tracks, it can cause the car to traction roll.

Decreasing ride height
Decreasing the front and rear ride height will make the car more aggressive, and decrease the ability of the car to soak up bumps. This is also suitable for high traction tracks, as the lower centre of gravity can minimize the chances of traction rolling.

— Ryan Maker

Ride Height Split

Setting the front ride height to be lower than the rear by approximately 0.5mm is a normal practice and provides:
- Increased corner entry steering.
- Increased stability in corners.

- Increased on-power oversteer and therefore reducing the difference between the front and rear ride heights will increase rear traction.

Increasing ride height split
Increasing the difference between front and rear ride height can have noticeable balance effects on the car. Lowering the front, or raising the rear; will cause the car to be more aggressive, especially entering corners and at high speed. This will give the car more steering and is generally more suitable on low traction tracks.

Decreasing ride height split
Decreasing the difference between front and rear ride height can smooth out an aggressive car, especially entering corners and at high speed. This will keep the car more stable and is generally suited to higher traction tracks, as it can reduce the chance of traction roll. Never run the rear ride height lower than the front.

— Ryan Maker

Starting Ride Height

The following are reasonable starting ride heights:

Track	Front	Rear
Carpet*	5mm	5.2mm
Asphalt	5mm	5.4mm

* Carpet tracks usually specify a minimum ride height to protect the carpet surface, this is often 5mm, but check with the race director.

Important: Measure ride height when the car is race-ready, including battery.

Measuring Ride Height

Ride height refers to the height of the chassis off the ground and is measured with a ride height gauge:

1. Place the car on a flat surface.
2. Push down and release the front and rear of the car a few times to settle the suspension.
3. Measure the ride height at the front and rear of the car at the lowest points of the chassis.

It can be difficult to measure the front ride height in the centre of the chassis because the bumper obscures your view. Therefore, slide the ride height gauge in between the bumper and the front suspension arm on the side. This gives a fairly accurate reading, unless your chassis is very worn. Check both sides and use the average if the ride height on each side is different:

Front Ride Height

Rear Ride Height

The Ride Height is not the measurement you can see on the gauge, but the adjacent one hidden underneath the chassis. E.g., for the rear height (above) the visible gauge is 5.6mm, but the chassis is too low for the 5.6mm step to fit. Therefore the chassis is actually at 5.4mm (the first step under the chassis).

Graphite chassis on asphalt tracks tend to wear in the locations we use to measure ride height. If your chassis is badly worn, then measure in a different location (I suggest on each side behind the front wheels and in front of the rear wheels) or use a ride height gauge with longer steps such as the RC Maker gauge below:

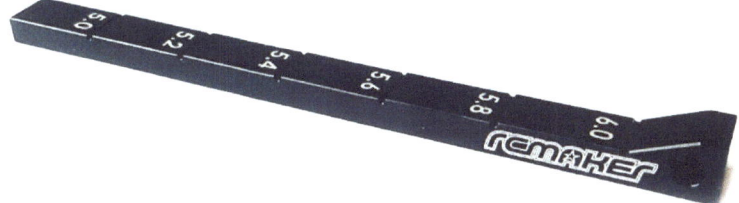

Left vs Right Side Ride Height

It is possible for the ride height on the left and right of the car to be different. Therefore we ideally measure in the centre of the chassis. However, if the difference between the sides is greater than 0.2mm, it can cause handling issues.

Possible causes:

- The left-to-right weight balance of the car may be different (refer page *155*).
- The shock springs may no longer be the same length and therefore need replacing.
- The shock preload may not be the same left-to-right (refer page *110*).
- The car's suspension may be Tweaked (refer page *165*).
- With foam tyres, the tyres may be different diameters left-to-right. This is also possible with rubber tyres, although less likely.

If, after working through the above list, you cannot identify the cause, then you can adjust the shock preload to correct it (refer to the procedure *Correcting Suspension Tweak* on page *168*).

Changing the Ride Height

Ride height is changed using shock preload. Refer to page *110*. Do not change ride height with the droop screws (refer to Droop on page *119*).

For more tips on setting Ride Height refer to page *75*.

Ride Height Interactions

Recheck the ride height whenever you:

- Change tyres.
- Finish a run on foam tyres.
- Change Droop (refer page 138) or Camber (refer page 98).
- After a crash.

Ride Heights interact. As you increase the front ride height, the rear ride height will reduce slightly and vice versa. After changing one end of the car always re-check the other end.

When ride height is changed, the following may be affected and should be checked:

- Camber.
- Toe.
- Droop. For instructions on changing Droop refer to page 118.

When you do this to Ride Height	Also do this to Droop	Notes
Increase	Increase	Increasing ride height will decrease droop
Decrease	Decrease	Decreasing ride height will increase droop

Ride Height and Tyres

When using rubber tyres, your ride height settings should stay fairly consistent, since rubber tyres do not lose significant diameter due to wear during use.

However, if using foam tyres, the car's ride height decreases as the foam tyres wear down to smaller diameters. Tyres may wear at different rates front-to-back, and left-to-right, which may eventually result in a car with uneven ride height at all four corners. For solutions to uneven wear with foam tyres refer to page 151.

Roll Bars

Level: Intermediate

Most cars have the option of Roll Bars, also called Anti-roll Bars or Torsion Bars.

Roll bars can limit the chassis roll while running slightly softer springs than would otherwise be possible, giving more steering going into a corner, more rear grip coming out of the corner and better stability and directional responsiveness.

While overall traction cannot be changed, roll bars allow the traction to be balanced. Increasing the stiffness of a roll bar on one axle decreases its traction and increases the traction of the axle at the other end of the car.

Chassis stiffness (page *103*) plays a very important role in the effectiveness of roll bars. A stiffer chassis makes the car more responsive to roll bar changes.

Roll Bar	Setting	Effect
Front	Thicker (stiffer)	• Reduces chassis roll. • Decreases front grip. • Increases rear grip. • Reduces off-power steering at corner entry, increasing understeer. • Faster steering response.
	Thinner (softer)	• Increases chassis roll. • Increases front grip. • Reduces rear grip. • Increases off-power steering at corner entry. • Slower steering response.
Rear	Thicker (stiffer)	• Reduces chassis roll. • Decreases rear grip. • Increases front grip. • Increases on-power steering. • Faster steering response in high-speed chicanes.
	Thinner (softer)	• Increases chassis roll. • Increases rear grip. • Reduces front grip. • Decreases on-power steering.

Before installation, lay the roll bar on a flat surface to ensure it is straight. Follow your car's manual for installation instructions.

Car Setup Reference

Roll bars are a good tuning option for changing the front-to-rear balance of the car. Usually you should adjust them independently, not both at the same time. Adjusting independently allows you to fine-tune the balance.

Front Roll Bar

Thicker will increase overall steering, most noticeably turn-in and high-speed. It makes the car edgy and more difficult to drive.

Thinner will decrease steering and make the car easier to drive. The front will be less twitchy and more stable at high speed.

Rear Roll Bar

Thicker will decrease on-power rear traction and off-power rotation.

Thinner will increase on-power rear traction and off-power rotation.

— Ryan Maker

Roll Bar Installation

Roll bars should be installed using the process on page *58*. After installation set the roll bar tweak using the process on page *71*.

Interaction

Chassis stiffness can significantly affect the effectiveness of roll bars. A stiffer chassis makes the car more responsive to roll bar changes. Refer to Chassis Stiffness on page *103*.

Roll Centre

Level: Advanced

The roll centre of the car is the imaginary point around which the car will roll when cornering. By adjusting the roll centre, we can make the car roll more or less and therefore increase or decrease the traction.

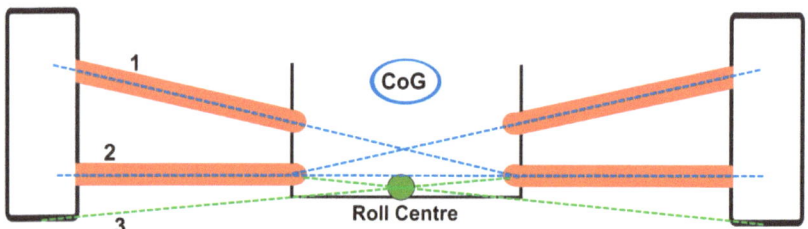

The illustration above shows the car from the front, including:
- The car's Centre of Gravity (CoG) (refer to page *157*).
- The Roll Centre (green circle).

To calculate the front roll centre when the car is stationary:

1. Draw blue dotted line (1) through the camber link.
2. Draw blue dotted line (2) through the suspension arm.
3. Where lines (1) and (2) meet is an imaginary point called the Instant Centre.
4. Draw green dotted line (3) from the Instant Centre to the middle of the tyre contact patch.
5. Repeat for the other side of the car.
6. Where the two green dotted lines meet is the Roll Centre.

When cornering, the car will roll as shown in the diagram on the right, with the Centre of Gravity (CoG) rolling around the roll centre.

By raising the height of the roll centre, the blue line becomes shorter. The car will therefore not roll as much and traction will be reduced. It will take less time to roll so the car will react to steering inputs more quickly.

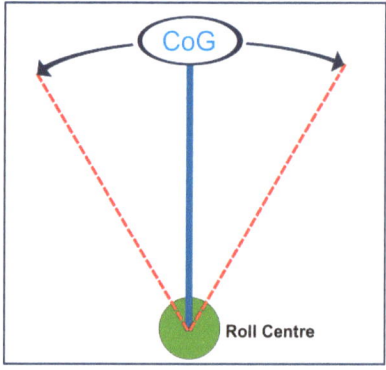

By lowering the height of the roll centre (above the track), the blue line becomes longer. Therefore, the car will roll more and traction will be increased. It will take more time to roll so the car will react slower to steering inputs and feels less responsive. Using a lower roll centre may assist to reduce traction rolling.

Changing the Roll Centre

The roll centre is determined by the relative angle between the camber links and suspension arms. To change this, some cars will use shims and some will use blocks (option parts may be required). Refer to your car's manual. Always make the same change to the left and right side of the car.

Should I Change the Suspension Arm Angle or the Camber Link Angle?

Both have the same effect. However, you may need to shim the camber link by 1mm or more to equate to a 0.5mm change on the suspension arms. The camber link is therefore often used for fine tuning the roll centre.

Front Roll Centre	Change By	Effect
Lower	Lower the suspension arms towards the chassis or raise the **inside** camber links by adding shims	• Car rolls more at front. • Increases front traction. • More steering response. • More mid-corner and exit steering.
Higher	Raise the suspension arms away from the chassis or raise the **outside** camber links by adding shims	• Car rolls less at front. • Decreases front traction. • Less steering response. • Less mid-corner and exit steering.

Rear Roll Centre	Change By	Effect
Lower	Lower the suspension arms towards the chassis or raise the **inside** camber links by adding shims	• Car rolls more at rear. • Increases rear traction. • Increases forward traction. • More mid-corner and exit steering. • Best for low grip tracks.
Higher	Raise the suspension arms away from the chassis or raise the **outside** camber links by adding shims	• Car rolls less at rear. • Decreases rear traction. • Decreases forward traction. • Less steering response. • Easier to drive. • Better in chicanes. • Best for high grip tracks.

The front suspension has a different roll centre to the rear suspension.
- Any changes made to the left front should also be made to the right front.
- Any changes made to the left rear should also be made to the right rear.

> There are also variations of roll centre such as Anti-dive, and Anti-squat which sets the suspension arms on an angle. I find flat suspension arms are the best; you can get very lost when exploring all these different variations. Keep it simple!
> — Ryan Maker

Roll centre is a complex area of vehicle mechanics and has been simplified here. If you are reading other texts on roll centre, then you may find it helpful to know that it is the geometric roll centre described above (vehicle is stationary). When the suspension is compressed or lifted, the roll centre will move and the roll centre at any point in time is called the instantaneous roll centre. How much the roll centre moves when the suspension compresses is determined by the relative angle between the top and bottom arms, and the arm length. Some cars provide optional mounting points for the camber links in order to change the link length.

Interaction

Lowering the roll centre by increasing the angle of the front camber link will slightly increase the Camber Gain (refer to page *101*).

Rollout

Refer to *Gearing & Rollout* on page *126*.

Shock Absorber

Refer to Damping on page *105*.

Solid Axle (Spool)
Level: Basic

A solid axle, also known as a spool, is often used at the front of the car (instead of a differential). A solid axle means that the left and right tyres rotate at the same speed at all times.

Solid axles reduce car weight. The drawback is less off-power steering.

A differential can be used instead of a solid axle (refer to page *115*). A front diff will provide less steering response, but more overall steering and cornering speed compared to a solid axle.

A one-way front axle was popular in the past, but makes the car significantly harder to drive and has therefore fallen out of favour.

Steering Arm Ball-cup Location

Refer to *Ackermann* on page *90*.

Steering Linkage Angle

Refer to Bump Steer on page *97*.

Steering Throw/Lock

Level: Basic

The turning radius of the car should be the same to the left as it is to the right. If you have a setup station, follow its instruction manual to test this. If not, you can test this by:

1. Place your race ready car on a flat surface with the body off (wheels on).
2. Make sure the car is located safely (or remove the pinion gear) in case you touch the throttle trigger by mistake.
3. Turn on the transmitter and then turn on your car.
4. Turn the steering all the way to the left and then all the way to the right. Check that the wheels don't rub on the arms or chassis.
5. Adjust your transmitter's steering servo End Point Adjustment (EPA) so that both left and right wheels turn the same amount. NB: When adjusting EPA first check that the Dual Rate on the radio is set to 100%.

The wheels should turn equally in both directions for balanced handling.

Pro drivers often reduce the Steering Throw (also called Steering Lock) to maximise corner speed. You can see examples of this in the Case Studies chapter on page *172* (the angle referred to is the inside wheels steering angle at full lock).

Toe

Level: Basic

Toe-out is when the front of the wheel points away from the centreline of the car. Conversely, toe-in is when the front of the wheel points in towards the centreline of the car.

The greater the toe angle the greater the friction and therefore the lower the top speed. However, adding toe can stabilise the car. So you want to use the smallest toe angle possible while making the car easy to drive.

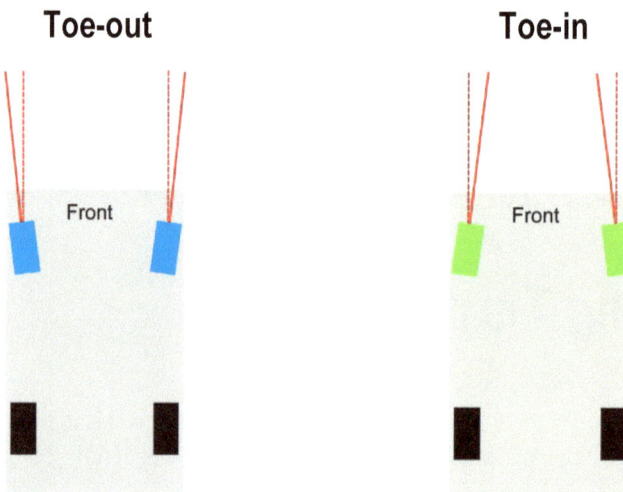

Measuring Toe

We recommend using a toe gauge. Toe is measured as an angle (in degrees) and therefore it is very difficult to measure front toe without one, although rear toe is often set using fixed blocks or shims.

However, if you must set front toe without a toe gauge, it can be done by measuring between the front of the wheels (red line) and the rear of the wheels (green line). Adjust the length of the Steering Linkages so that the red line is 1mm longer than the green line. Make sure the left and right Steering Linkages are equal in length.

Front Toe Angle

A good starting point is front toe-out of 1 degree. Front toe-in is not recommended.

If you have just built your car, set the Steering Throw (refer to page *144*) before setting the front Toe.

There is a great deal of confusion about front toe and its effects. To ensure this book contains the most accurate information, the following table was collated by interviewing several world and national champions:

Front Toe	Change	Effect
Toe-out	Increase (more toe-out)	• Car more stable on the straight. • Decreases steering (most noticeable at corner entry). • Less steering response. • Makes car easier to drive. • Car more prone to understeer.
	Decrease (less toe-out)	• Car less stable on the straight. • Increases steering. • More steering response. • Car is harder to drive. • Less prone to understeer.
Neutral Toe	Tyres straight	• Fastest straight line speed. However, less than 0.5 degree of toe-out is not recommended.
Toe-in	Not recommended.	

Front Toe

Toe can be a very important tool for finding the correct balance on the car. You should always use toe-out at the front.

Increasing front toe-out will smooth the car's steering response. This is especially good for high traction, when the car is twitchy around neutral. It will also slightly decrease on-power steering and steering on sweepers.

Decreasing front toe-out will make the car more edgy and aggressive entering a corner. This can be good for low traction in order to get aggression out of the car. It will also increase high-speed steering and on-power steering.

— *Ryan Maker*

Rear Toe Angle

A good starting point is rear toe-in of 3 degrees.

Rear Toe	Change	Effect
Toe-in	Increase (more toe-in)	• Increases traction. • More stable. • Greater understeer on-power. • Less cornering speed.
	Decrease (less toe-in)	• Reduces traction. • Less stable. • More cornering speed. • More on-power steering. • Better rotation.
Toe-out	Never used.	

In general, the more rear toe-in, the more stable your car will be. The rear wheels of your race car should always be adjusted with some toe-in. Rear toe-out is never used.

Increasing the angle of rear toe-in will cause decreased straight line speed, but the car will be more stable. Rear toe-in must be the same on the left and right side of the car.

Rear Toe

Increasing rear toe-in will give the car more rear traction overall. At slow speed, the extra toe can increase rotation and low-speed steering; particularly noticeable on hairpins. More rear toe is generally used on lower traction tracks where the car suffers from instability, especially on-power.

Decreasing rear toe-in will give the car less rear traction overall. If the traction is high, then this can give the car more corner speed and free it up through corners. If you use less rear toe-in low traction, it can make the rear quite unstable, making it hard to get on the power.

Active Rear Toe

Active rear toe is commonly found on modern day touring cars and instead of a fixed rear toe block, there is now a setup similar to the steering, with fixed steering links. The purpose of this is to adjust the rear toe depending on where the weight is transferred on the car. This setting can be altered by adjusting the angle of the toe links that connect from the inner bulkhead to the outer hub on the active rear toe.

Generally active toe is only increased under compression. A typical setting would be 3 degrees toe increasing to 3.3–3.5 degrees under compression, and we change this by changing the shims under the link on the rear steering hub. More shims = less toe gain, less shims = more toe gain. This aspect of the car is very track dependent, so I recommend you try many combinations at your track. Generally, you will use more toe gain on low grip, and less toe gain on high grip. Active rear toe can be a disadvantage on small low traction tracks as it makes the car very difficult and inconsistent to drive, due to the abrupt movement of the car.

More Toe Gain
More toe gain is an adjustment to the toe link that results in a bigger increase in toe under compression. This results in increased stability, especially on-power. This also means that since the toe change is more abrupt than before, when the car unloads it will change its handling characteristic more, leading to random snapping when the weight transfers to the front, as the toe reduction is more significant. This setting is generally better for lower traction, flowing tracks to get good drive out of corners and carry corner speed. On tracks with lots of braking, accelerating and hairpins, this could be a disadvantage as the car will be inconsistent. Using this setting on high traction generally makes the car "hook" nastily and should be avoided.

Less Toe Gain
Less toe gain is an adjustment to the toe link that results in a smaller increase in toe under compression. This results in decreased stability on-power, however still has more than a standard, fixed rear end. This will, however, be more consistent because the difference between the toe under compression and the toe when the rear is unloaded is less. This setting is better for higher traction, small tracks with faster changes of direction and gives maximum steering from your active rear toe. Using this setting on low traction could lead to a loose rear end and an unpredictable, inconsistent car.

— *Ryan Maker*

Interaction

Changing the front Track Width will change the front toe setting.

If the front toe is adjusted, you should re-check your Steering Throw, refer to page *144*.

Track Width

Level: Intermediate

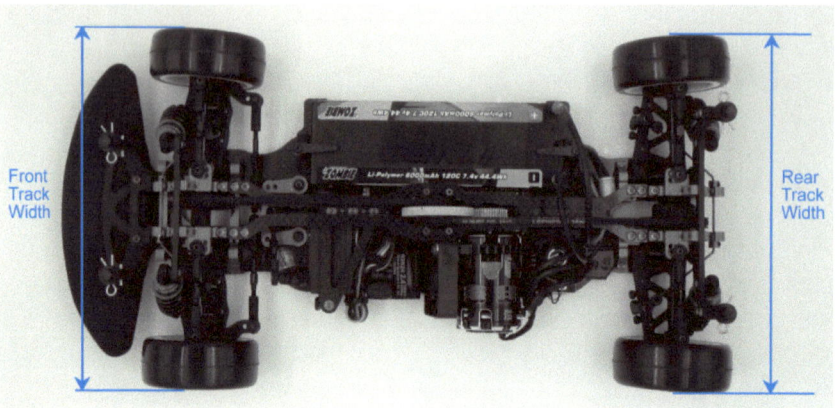

Track width is the distance between the outside edges of the wheels. Most racing classes will have rules specifying the maximum track width.

The track width at the front may be different to the rear. It is important when making a change that it is made to both the left and the right. I.e., the left and right wheels must be the same distance from the centreline of the chassis.

Track Width can be adjusted via:

- the inner suspension mounts, or
- through the width of the wheel hexes.

Front Track Width	Effect
Wider	• Decreases front grip. • Slower steering response. • Increases understeer. • Easier to drive. • Reduces traction rolling. • Better for high-grip tracks.
Narrower	• Increases front grip. • Faster steering response. • Decreases understeer. • Better for low-medium grip tracks.

Rear Track Width	Effect
Wider	• Increases car stability. • Easier to drive. • Increases rear grip at corner entry and mid corner. • More on-power understeer. • Decreases cornering speed. • Better for high-grip tracks.
Narrower	• Reduces car stability. • Increases car responsiveness. • Increases rear grip at corner exit. • Increases cornering speed. • Increases on-power steering. • Better for low-medium grip tracks.

Wheel Hexes

Narrow wheel hexes (less than 5mm) will decrease the cars track width and generate more traction. This will yield a more responsive and agile car. Narrow hexes, especially at the front, can increase high-speed steering and low-speed response. Narrow hexes at the rear can increase the rotation of the car, especially off-power in tight hairpins.

Wide wheel hexes (more than 5mm) will increase the cars track width and generate less traction. They will make the car easier to drive and more stable. Wider hexes, especially at the front, can be used to stop traction rolling in high traction conditions. Wider hexes at the rear allow you to get more forward traction and stability.

Suspension Blocks

Altering the track width from the suspension blocks effectively alters three things; different length turnbuckle, different shock position on the arm, and changing toe-in or toe-out on the front. This makes it a more substantial change than changing wheel hex width.

Wider

Widening the front will give the car less steering overall, especially in the middle and exit of the corner. It can be used to decrease tyre wear or decrease tyre heat. Widening the rear will make the car more stable off-power, with less rotation and less rear side bite on-power. However, it can increase the cars forward traction.

> **Narrower**
> Narrowing the front will give the car more overall steering, especially middle and exit of the corner. It will also give more steering at high speed. It can cause the car to traction roll on high traction tracks, and cause higher front tyre wear.
>
> Narrowing the rear will increase the cars rotation off-power, and increase rear side bite on-power. It can cause the car to traction roll on high traction tracks because it makes the rear of the car more active and aggressive.
>
> — Ryan Maker

Interaction

Changing the front Track Width will change the front Toe setting (refer to page *145*).

Tyres & Additives
Level: Basic

The correct tyre choice is critical to your setup. Most major races will specify control tyres so that all racers are on an even playing field. However, if you have the choice of tyres, then ask the local fast drivers what they are using.

This section is not a guide to tyre selection; rather, it provides information on getting the most from the tyres you use.

As a general rule, the softer the tyres are, the more grip they will provide. However, the softer the tyre, the greater the likelihood of overheating on a hot track.

Tyres may come unglued from the wheels and should be checked after each run and re-glued if necessary.

Rubber Tyres

Rubber tyres are the norm in touring car racing.

When using rubber tyres, your ride height settings should stay consistent, since they do not reduce in diameter significantly from run to run. The wear on rubber tyres affects grip but rarely causes the issues listed for foam below.

Rubber tyres are more likely to come unglued from the wheels than foam and should be checked after each run and re-glued if necessary.

Rubber tyres on outside asphalt are more susceptible to track temperature changes than rubber tyres on carpet.

For examples of rubber tyre usage refer to the Case Studies chapter beginning on page 172.

Foam Tyres

Foam tyres are rarely used in touring car racing.

Tyre warmers are not required with foam tyres. However, on low grip surfaces, they may assist the traction additive to soften the tyres and therefore generate additional grip.

Foam tyres are not as susceptible to track temperature changes as rubber tyres.

As foam tyres wear, the reduction in diameter means you should check after each run:

- **Ride Height** (refer to page 134) — The car's ride height decreases as the foam tyres wear down to smaller diameters. Tyres may wear at different rates front-to-back and left-to-right, because the track may have more corners, or high-speed corners, in one direction. This may lead to a car with uneven ride height at all four corners. If necessary, swap tyres left-to-right to maintain even wear. Some racers will use a tyre truer to maintain even ride height.

- **Gearing** (refer to Rollout on page 128).

- **Tyre Coning** i.e., either the inside or outside of the tyre is wearing at a faster rate causing the tyre to "cone". Check Camber and adjust as necessary to promote even wear across the surface of the tyre and prevent coning (refer to page 98).

Check after each run that tyres remain firmly glued to the rims and re-glue if necessary.

Tyre Preparation

One of the hardest things to perfect for all levels of drivers, from club racers to World Champions, is tyre preparation. I can't stress enough how crucial it is to prepare your tyres properly! That means everything from mounting and gluing; to the moment you put your car on the track.

Always use oil based cleaners. Many companies make specific tyre cleaners which you can test. The Volante Tyre Essence is a perfect example, and both yellow and blue work extremely well. The easiest and most consistent solution is to use Würth brand brake cleaner. You also need a good cloth to use for cleaning tyres. I highly recommend Scott Shop Towels from Costco. To clean the tyres well, leave them attached to the car and use a wheel nut spanner to turn the wheel, while you wipe the tyre with Würth on your cloth. You should be able to remove any excess black rubber on used tyres, or release agent on new tyres.

Cleaning the tyre with additive is also a popular procedure and can leave more oil in the tyre than using Würth. Test it for yourself and see what works for you.

You will notice that most tyres have a centre mould line when they are new. Not removing this can affect the tyres performance for the first few laps. Remove this line with a special tool such as the Tyre Line Remover from RC Maker (pictured below). It features a V-shaped cutter which can remove the whole bead without heat cycling the tyre (occurs when using a tyre sander). Make sure you do this before cleaning the tyres.

When cleaning tyres, try not to touch them too much during and after as your finger grease can affect the surface traction. If it happens, you should re-clean your tyres before applying additive.

— *Ryan Maker*

Additive

Additive softens the tyre and increases grip. Normally a track's grip will increase during the race meeting as rubber and additive are laid down on the track and track temperature increases. This may mean reducing the application of additive as the meeting progresses to maintain the level of grip for which you have set up your car.

Additive is normally applied some time before the race and allowed to soak into the tyres, softening the rubber. How long before depends on the tyre compound, the additive, the track surface and temperature, air temperature and whether tyre warmers are used. However, leaving the additive on for at least 15 minutes is a good starting point. Manufacturers produce different additive products for asphalt and carpet tracks.

It is normal to apply additive across the entire surface of the rear tyres and to some or all of the front tyres, depending on how much steering is needed. If applying additive only to a portion of the front tyre, then always start at the inside of the tyre (the part closest to the chassis) as this part of the tyre should be touching the track before the car starts to turn in (assuming negative Camber, refer page 98) and should continue to touch the track throughout the turn. Whereas the outside of the tyre might only touch the track close to the corner apex.

For examples of additive usage, refer to the Case Studies chapter beginning on page 172.

> Many people drown their tyres in additive and expect them to be sticky when they pull them off the warmers — wrong! The trick is to use enough additive to cover the tyre, but only as a thin film and not too thick and wet. I put an even coat directly onto the tyre from the additive bottle, then I take a cloth and just lightly wipe any excess so there is a nice thin film. This way it can mostly evaporate by the time you race.
>
> You want to make sure the tyres are tacky when they come off the tyre warmers; if they aren't, then you probably don't have the right additive for the particular tyre you are using.
>
> There's no rule on which additive you should use in the cold, but often a thinner, less oily additive is the best option.
>
> In hot conditions you should use a thicker, oily additive, so you may need to wipe the tyres after you take the warmers off. You want the tyre relatively dry and tacky when you hit the track.

Here are some additives I generally use for high and low traction. They can be used in cold and warm conditions if prepared correctly (as recommended above):

High Traction: Volante Purple, Nasa Mighty Gripper V3 Yellow or Red, MR33 V4, or LRP Carpet 3.

Low Traction: Volante Purple, Spider Grip Orange, Gravity RC LG2, Trinity Tire Tweak, or MR33 V3 Outdoor.

— Ryan Maker

Tyre Warmers

Tyre warmers have two primary uses:

1. Warm rubber tyres to their operating temperature so they provide good grip as soon as the car is placed on the track. If you do not use tyre warmers, then you will need to do some warm-up laps to heat the tyres before the race.

2. To improve the absorption of additive. By heating the tyre while the additive is absorbed, the additive should soften the tyre to a greater degree than without tyre warmers.

For examples of tyre warmer usage refer to the Case Studies chapter beginning on page *172*.

Many people like to use tissues in the warmer cups, however I find that this prevents the tyre from getting 'tacky'. A better approach is to use minimal additive without tissues, then wipe the tyre dry before racing if necessary.

Cold weather:

In cold weather you must keep the tyres warm right up until your race starts. Warm on 60°C (140°F) for 10–15 minutes before your race, and take the warmers off as late as possible before your race. This ensures the heat stays in the tyre and you don't have to do more than one warm up lap to warm your tyres. Excessive warm up laps compromises your increased pace at the start of a race by wearing off the additive.

If the traction is high, you may not want to warm for quite so long, as this will cause the tyre to over grip.

Hot weather:

Most people don't think you need tyre warmers when it is hot; this is a common misconception. In a lot of cases the warmers are used to infuse the additive into the tyre, not actually to keep the tyres warm for your race. In hot conditions, I will use tyre warmers 90% of the time, at 60°C (140°F) for about 15 minutes, taking them off about 5 minutes before my race to let the tyres cool.

There are very specific conditions when the track is super hot and super high traction, that using warmers at all can be detrimental, as it will over grip the car and heat the tyres up faster.

— *Ryan Maker*

Wheel Balancing

When installing a new set of tyres, pro racers often check the wheel balance. If a wheel is significantly out of balance, they might add lead tape to ensure the wheel runs true. Unbalanced wheels can affect the perfect handling of your car. However, if the wheel is not too unbalanced, then it is common to not balance it. Check whether wheel balancing is allowed under the race meeting rules.

Weight

Level: Basic

Most racing classes have a minimum weight rule where the race ready car must be at least that weight. Depending on your car, battery, motor and electronics choices, this may mean it is necessary to add weight, or you may be looking for ways to reduce weight.

A heavy car will usually have more traction than a lighter car. However, a lighter car will be faster than a heavy car. Because our goal is the fastest possible lap-time, we normally run the car as close to the minimum weight as possible and change the setup of the car to provide the traction needed.

It can be risky to run too close to the weight limit, as cars found to be underweight after the race may be disqualified. Foam tyre wear may reduce the weight of the car slightly.

If you need to add weight, then do so as low on the chassis as possible and check that the car remains balanced left-to-right. Both of these are explained below.

Centre of Gravity

The Centre of Gravity (CoG) of the car is the balance point of the mass of the car. The lower the CoG, the better. This is achieved by placing all electronics as low as possible on the chassis and minimising any weight high up.

The higher the CoG, the more the car will roll in a corner. It is better to keep the CoG as low as possible and change the Roll Centre to increase chassis roll if required (refer to page *141*).

Weight Balance (Side-to-Side)

Ideally:

1. The weight on your front left tyre should be the same as the weight on your front right tyre, and
2. The weight on your rear left tyre should be the same as the weight on your rear right tyre.

You should always try to adjust the weight on your chassis, so it is equal left-to-right. It doesn't have to be perfect but should be within 10g (0.02 pounds) left-to-right. This will assist with consistent handling, and to keep the ride height similar on both sides of the chassis. It is easiest to do this while building the kit.

There are two main methods to achieve this. For both, make sure your pit board is perfectly flat by checking it with a spirit level (sometimes called a water level). Otherwise, the weight balance reading might not be accurate.

1. Balancing Tool

Manufacturers will often provide a hole in the chassis at the front and rear of the car to check left-to-right weight balance. Imagine two nails sticking up from your pit table and the car balancing on these nails (one nail per hole in the chassis). You can buy a tool such as the one below from MR33.

2. Individual Scales

Individual scales show the weight supported by each tyre

The disadvantage of using scales is that you are measuring the sprung weight of the car, and the springs can introduce a variable. To eliminate this variable, use shock restrictors like those from RC Maker below, giving a more accurate reading.

Weight Balancing

If your car is heavier on one side, then move the electronics/battery, or add weight, so that the car sits level.

Many manufacturers will allow the servo, and/or the battery to be shifted to the right or left side of the car to assist with weight balance. However, it is optimum to have these as close to the chassis centreline as possible.

Due to their construction, lipo batteries may be slightly lighter on the plug end.

A small amount of lead weight can be added to one side to balance the car if required. Modern cars are often underweight out of the box and require weight to be added.

Some classes, such as Vintage Trans Am, require a lot of weight to be added to meet the minimum weight rule. In this case add the weight as low down and as centrally as possible. MR33 make a range of weights for this purpose, such as this one for placing under the battery:

Moving Weight (Front-to-Rear)

Re-distributing existing weight can be a useful tuning tool. This is most easily done by moving the battery location (refer to page 95).

> When it comes to moving weight, we can position it in order to fine-tune the handling of the car.
>
> **Weight at the rear** will increase the cars on-power rear traction initially under acceleration, as well as increase steering into corners and at high speed. It can make the car quite difficult to drive, causing traction rolling in high grip and snap oversteer in low grip.
>
> **Weight at the front** will decrease steering into corners, decrease steering at high speed, but add stability. It will make the car easier to drive, especially in high traction, where traction rolling is an issue. It will be more predictable in low traction and reduce the car's aggression and steering capabilities.
>
> — *Ryan Maker*

Adding Weight to Increase Steering or Rear Traction

Car handling is determined by weight transfer (refer to page 23). However, the car should be kept as close to the minimum weight for the class as possible.

Adding weight to the front for more steering, or to the rear to increase rear grip, *does not work*. This is because it is the transfer of weight to one end of the car that changes car handling.

If you take any car and double its weight, then it will not be able to take the corner as quickly because it must change the direction of the additional weight. Adding physical weight to the rear of the car to correct oversteer could make the car oversteer even more because the car must now change the direction of this extra weight when cornering. As a general rule, the lighter your car, the better it will corner.

Although static weight certainly impacts handling, it should only be added in extremely slippery conditions such as a wet or extremely low grip track. When adding static weight, make sure your car remains balanced left-to-right (as above), and add the weight as low down and as close to the centreline as possible.

To increase steering without adding weight, refer to the checklist on page 258.

To increase rear traction without adding weight, refer to the checklist on page 254.

If after reading this you still want to add weight at one end of the car, then I recommend no more than 10–15g (.02–.03 pounds).

Wheelbase

Level: Advanced

Wheelbase is the distance between the front and rear axle. The greater the distance, the longer the wheelbase, the shorter the distance, the shorter the wheelbase. Most cars have the option of changing the wheelbase, refer to your car's manual.

By adjusting the wheelbase at one end of the car, you affect the traction at that end. For example, by shortening the wheelbase at the rear of the car, you place more weight over the rear wheels (resulting in more rear traction.)

Wheelbase	Effect
Longer	- More stability. - Easier to drive. - Less steering response. - Better for larger tracks. - Better for high traction tracks. - Better for longer corners (sweepers).
Shorter	- Less stable. - More difficult to drive. - Better for tight technical tracks. - Better for tracks with many 180 degree corners. - The car rotates better in the centre of the corner. - Car carries more corner speed.

The front wheelbase usually has less adjustability than the rear wheelbase. It is a good tuning option to change the weight position over the tyres to fine-tune the car's balance.

Lengthening wheelbase

Lengthening the **front** wheelbase will increase the car's steering initially and corner speed in sweepers. However, it can make the car "wash out" mid-corner and understeer.

Lengthening the **rear** wheelbase will make the car more stable in general and decrease rotation or snap oversteer.

Car Setup Reference 6

Shortening wheelbase

Shortening the **front** wheelbase will decrease the car's initial steering, but will increase the overall steering and rotation of the car at low speed.

Shortening the **rear** wheelbase will increase the car's rotation, especially on slower corners such as hairpins. It generates more forward traction as it allows more weight transfer over the rear end.

— *Ryan Maker*

Wings

Refer to page 87.

162

Chapter 7

Tweak

What is Tweak?

Tweak is the adjustment of the suspension so that both rear tyres touch the ground with equal pressure, and both front tyres touch the ground with equal pressure.

A "tweaked" car displays inconsistent handling. For example, it may turn to one side when accelerating in a straight line, or it may oversteer on one corner and understeer at the next.

Tweak Checklist

A "tweaked" car may be caused by:

1. Build Error/Setup Error

1. **Left and right settings unequal** — Settings on the left of the car are different to settings on the right. Check:

    a. Droop screws may not be set the same left-to-right. Refer to page *119*.

    b. Shock length may not be the same left-to-right. Refer to page *106*.

    c. Shock spring preload may be different left-to-right. Refer to page *110*. Although we may adjust preload later to correct tweak, it should start the same left-to-right.

    d. Other Damping settings may not be the same left-to-right. Refer to page *105*.

    e. Shims or physical parts may not be the same on the left and right sides.

2. **Binding parts** — Make sure that all suspension components move freely without binding including suspension arms and hinge pins, pivotballs, ball cups, etc.

3. **Twisted chassis** — Top deck, bulkhead or motor mount screws have been tightened inconsistently or using an incorrect pattern. See *Testing for Chassis Twist* below.

2. Crash Damage

1. **Physical Damage** — Cracked carbon fibre or plastic parts can cause unpredictable handling when the parts flex under load.

2. **Bent roll bars** — Check that they are flat. Refer to Roll Bar Installation on page *140* for installation and setting roll bar tweak.

3. **Twisted chassis** — components that are screwed to the chassis may move slightly in a crash, causing the chassis to twist. See *Testing for Chassis Twist* below.

3. Suspension Tweak

Ryan Maker describes this as follows:

> Suspension tweak is translated through your shock absorbers. It is noticeable when the chassis is sitting on an angle at ride height, with the shock collars wound down the same amount left-to-right.
>
> It causes the droop (up travel above ride height) to feel different on each side, even though when measured on the droop blocks it is the same. Often people will never notice this, but it is critical to making your car drive absolutely perfectly. There are a number of reasons this can occur:
>
> 1. **Shock tower machining is slightly misaligned** — The shock tower sits on a slight angle or the holes are not perfectly located where the shocks mount.
>
> 2. **Shock springs vary in length** — In a perfect world, shock springs would be identically matched in length. While some company's springs are quite good, some can be out by 0.1–0.3mm, which is enough to throw the ride height and tweak out a lot.
>
> 3. **Suspension blocks slightly off centre** — In some extreme cases, the suspension blocks may not be drilled in the perfect spot on the chassis and could cock the arms to one side, effectively making one shock have more distance to travel than the other. We are only talking 0.1–0.2mm, but it all adds up!
>
> In a perfect world, all of this would be absolutely spot on, but often it is not.

Refer to *Correcting Suspension Tweak* below.

Testing for Chassis Twist

Components that are screwed to the chassis might move in a crash and cause the chassis to twist, tweaking the car. Here are two methods for identifying this problem:

Method 1 — Quick Test

With the car race ready but body off, turn the car over and hold the chassis in your hand. Place a straight edge, such as a steel ruler, against the bottom of the chassis from the front left corner to the rear right corner. The ruler should be flush against the bottom of the chassis (make sure it is not catching on a protruding screw). Repeat for the opposite corners. If the ruler is not flush against the bottom of the chassis, then it is tweaked:

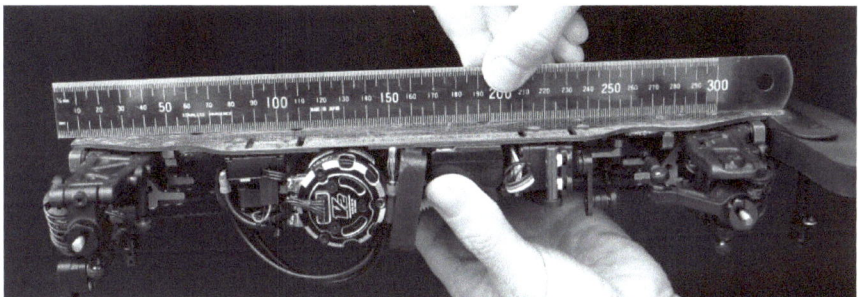

Method 2 — Detailed Test

1. Take off the wheels.

2. Place the car on a surface which is perfectly flat, a pit setup board or sheet of glass is ideal. If using a pit table or other surface which should be flat, then check it first with a steel ruler. If any gaps show between the ruler and the surface, then it is not perfectly flat.

3. Push down on opposite corners of the chassis and see if it rocks (front left and rear right, next try front right and rear left). The car should be perfectly flat on the surface, if it rocks, then double-check that the chassis isn't rocking on something like a protruding screw head or battery tape. If the chassis is flat on the surface but it still rocks, then the chassis is tweaked.

Un-twisting the Chassis

If the chassis is tweaked, then one or more of the components attached to the chassis may have moved:

1. Loosen all the screws under the chassis slightly (say half a turn) i.e., screws mounting the servo, front suspension arms, chassis bulkheads or uprights. This should remove the tension causing the tweak.

2. Gently tighten the screws using the following pattern:

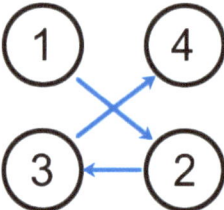

3. Before fully tightening the screws, re-check the chassis to see if it sits flat (the screws should be tight enough to not interfere with the chassis sitting flat, but not completely tight).

    a. If it sits flat, then proceed to step d below.

    b. If it doesn't sit flat, then there may be components secured to the chassis from the top which are tweaked, therefore:

        i. Loosen the top deck screws (and any chassis stiffeners, if installed).

        ii. With one hand, use a ruler to push down on both shock towers so that the chassis sits flat and does not rock.

        iii. With the other hand, gently tighten the top deck screws using the pattern in step 2 above.

        iv. Re-check the chassis to see if it sits flat. If it does, proceed to step d below.

    c. Sometimes the servo can twist slightly. Loosen the screws holding the servo in place and see if the chassis now sits flat. If it does, proceed to step d.

    d. Fully tighten the screws using the pattern in step 2 above. Re-check the chassis to see if it sits flat. If it does, then you have removed the tweak from your chassis. If it doesn't, then possibilities include: you have over-tightened screws, or tightened them in the wrong order, or a bulkhead or other component has been bent or damaged, or the chassis or top deck is damaged.

Correcting Suspension Tweak

Remember that both rear tyres should touch the ground with equal pressure, and both front tyres should touch the ground with equal pressure. If this is not the case, we must identify and correct it.

You should have gone through the checklist at the beginning of this chapter before trying these options, or you may obtain false results.

Below are options for identifying and fixing this issue, with and without specialist equipment:

Option 1 — When Tyres Leave the Ground

1. Check that your camber, droop and ride height are set correctly. If you're uncertain whether your roll bars are set correctly, then disconnect them.
2. Place your car, race ready, on a level surface (check it with a spirit level, if the surface is not level then the test will provide false results).
3. Settle the car on its suspension (tap both ends of the car with your finger).
4. With your eyes level with this surface, use a hex driver under the centre of the chassis to lift up one end of the car (front or rear). Most cars have a hole in the exact centre of the chassis that you can place your driver into.

In the example above the right rear tyre left the ground first

168

5. As the car lifts up, the wheels should come off the ground at exactly the same time. If one wheel leaves the ground before the other, there is a problem. In our example photo (above) the rear right wheel left the ground slightly before the rear left. This means the rear left has more pressure on it than the rear right. We need to even up this pressure. Correct this by:

   a) Change the shock preload on the other end of the car by screwing down the collar diagonally opposite the wheel that leaves the ground early (as shown in the example photo on the right). Adjust the same on both sides, e.g., if you screw down the front left by 1/8th of a turn, then unscrew the front right by 1/8th of a turn.

   b) Re-test from step 3 above.

   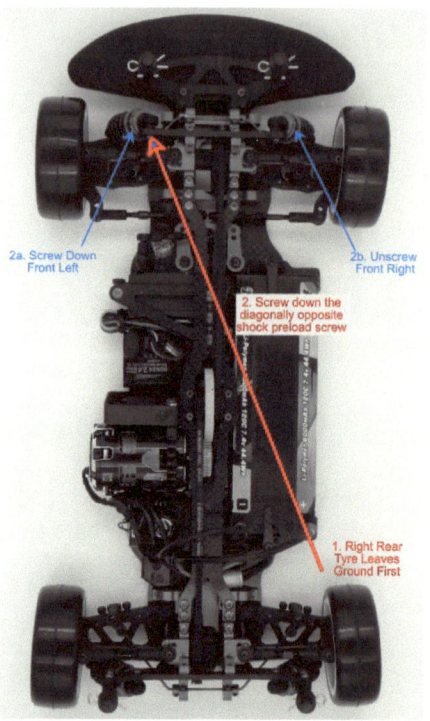

   NB: Excessive difference left-to-right — If the preload on the left and right sides of the car are different by more than 1.5mm (between front left and front right shocks, or between rear left and rear right shocks) then this is too much and could be because the shock tower has been tightened on an angle ("shock tower tweak"). Loosen the shock tower screws, twist the shock tower towards the side where the shock collar is screwed down more, and re-tighten. After doing this, you should now be able to back off that shock collar and tighten the opposite side, evening them up. Re-test from step 3 above.

6. Once one end of the car is set, proceed to test the other end from step 3 above. E.g., if you first tested the rear of the car, now test the front.

7. The up-travel on the front and the rear should now be perfect, with both left and right tyres leaving the ground at exactly the same time. If not, then this could be because your weight distribution is slightly wrong, and you may need to add weight to balance your car (refer to page 157). However, unless the weight balance is significantly out, the procedure above will solve all of your tweak issues!

8. Assuming you changed the shock preload to correct the tweak, then you will need to set your ride height again. Do this normally (refer to page 134) by

turning both left and right collars the same amount. Your ride height should now be the same on the left side of the car as on the right.

Optional Equipment

The above method requires no specialist equipment. However, rubber tyres may make it difficult to tell when a wheel is leaving the ground (wheels and tyres could be a slightly different size left-to-right.) For a more accurate test, if you have a setup station then attach the setup wheels to the end of the car that you are testing. Alternatively, RC Maker's Tweak Wheel Set makes it far easier to feel when one wheel is lifting up earlier:

Another handy bit of kit is the RC Maker Shock Restrictor Set. If after step 5a above, you find that the preload on the left and right sides of the car are different by more than 1.5mm then this is too far out and this could be because the shock tower has been tightened on an angle ("shock tower tweak"). The Shock Restictor Set simplifies the troubleshooting process by allowing you to check for shock tower tweak first, before adjusting the shock collars.

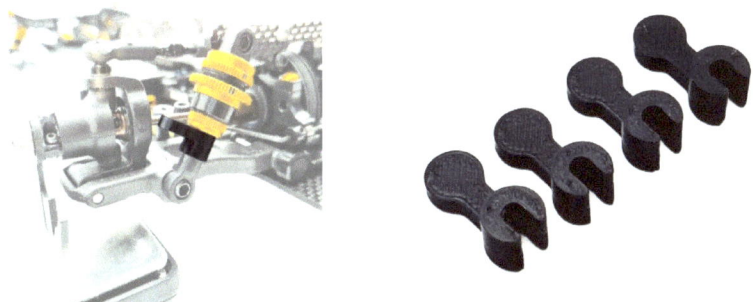

Installing the Shock Restrictors makes the resting distance between all four shocks fixed, isolating them and putting all readings through to the shock tower. Once these are installed, you can simply lift either end of the car (refer to step 4 above) to check the tweak of the opposite end's shock tower, and vice versa. Once the tweak is detected, simply loosen the shock tower screws and twist the correct way to bring the opposite end wheels into leaving the ground at the same time. Now that you've eliminated shock tower tweak, remove the Restrictors and put the springs back on. Now re-test from step 3 above.

The Restrictors also make side-to-side weight balancing (page *157*) much easier.

Option 2 — Tweak Station

Some manufacturers including MR33 and Hudy offer a tweak station which uses a spirit level, or measurement under the wheels, to determine tweak.

Using a tweak station should be done only after all other items on the checklist at the start of this chapter have been checked and corrected.

Follow the instruction manual that came with the tweak station to correct tweak by adjusting shock spring preload.

If the preload on the left and right sides of the car are different by more than 1.5mm, then this is too far out and you should re-visit the checklist at the start of this chapter to identify the root cause. Incorrectly adjusted spring preload can cause one side of the car being firmer or higher than the other, causing handling differences when turning left or right.

Chapter 8

Case Studies

Essential Touring Car RC Racer's Guide

This chapter describes actual race meetings and how skilled drivers approached their setup, what changes they made, why, and how car performance improved.

Different cars have unique handling characteristics. Even with the same chassis, driver style varies. That is why it is not recommended that you copy a world champion's car setup without understanding the settings. Instead, identify the differences between the world champion's setup and your car's setup and make one change at a time. Determine whether your car handles better or worse, based on your skill level and driving style, and fine-tune from there.

Carpet Case Studies

Starting Setup

If you have not raced at a particular track before, then we recommend starting with your chassis manufacturer's base carpet setup. You may also wish to search your chassis manufacturer's website for another driver's setup at that track so you can note the changes they made. We do not recommend using another driver's setup without knowing why they made the changes they did. However, it can be very useful to note the differences to the manufacturer's base carpet setup and then try each change, one at a time, and note whether it feels better or worse.

Changes Compared to Asphalt

1. Carpet tracks tend to be much smoother than asphalt and therefore you should set the ride height as low as practical. Check the minimum ride height allowed by the scrutineers. Make sure chassis screws are not protruding, as they might catch on the carpet. Depending on the track, sticky rubber residue might build up on the bottom of the chassis. If it does, raising the ride height slightly may prevent this.
2. Carpet generally provides more grip, and is less bumpy, than an asphalt track. The car can, therefore, be much stiffer while still providing sufficient grip. Refer to page *103* for how stiff you should make your car.
3. Tyre wear on carpet is significantly less than on asphalt.
4. Normally indoor tracks will have similar track temperatures throughout the day.

Case Studies 8

Case Study Track

Grand Prix des 3 Frontieres (GP3F), MRC Longwy, France. Medium grip carpet. Mixed track with both fast and technical sections.

Track Temperature

19°C (66°F).

Control Tyre

Volante R28.

Control Additive

Open. But all drivers below chose MR33 V4.

Special thanks to Kévin Thomassin Photographies for the GP3 photos.

Modified

Touring Car World Champions in this race: Marc Rheinard, Ronald Völker, Bruno Coelho and 1/12th World Champion Alexander Hagberg.

1st Ronald Völker (Yokomo), 2nd Marc Rheinard (Awesomatix), 3rd Yannic Prümper (Awesomatix), 4th Christopher Krapp (Yokomo), 5th Elliott Harper (Xray), 6th Bruno Coelho (Xray), 7th Dionys Stadler (Awesomatix), 8th Alexander Hagberg (Xray), 9th Marco Kaufmann (Xray), 10th Loic Jasmin (Awesomatix)

1st — Ronald Völker — Yokomo BD10

The following settings were left as per the manufacturer's basic carpet setup:

- Diff position front and rear is up (high).
- Diff oil is 7,500 cSt.
- Aluminium chassis.

Ronald's normal carpet setup is different to the manufacturer's basic carpet setup as follows:

- Front ride height increased from 5.0mm to 5.1mm, and rear ride height increased from 5.2mm to 5.3mm. To provide a little more clearance.
- Front camber increased from 1.5° to 2°. Rear camber decreased from 2.5° to 2°. These are my normal starting settings for camber.
- Front toe-out increased from 1° to 1.25°. This is my normal starting setting for front toe.

- Front droop increased from 4mm to 6mm (measured at front). This is my normal starting setting.
- Rear droop reduced from 3mm to 2mm (measured at centre side). 3mm of rear droop on the BD10 is equivalent to about 5.5mm on other brands.
- Front roll bar increased from 1.3 to 1.4mm. Makes the car easier to drive.
- Rear roll bar increased from 1.2 to 1.3mm. Provides better balance when using the 1.4mm front roll bar.
- Steering lock limited to 25°. Provides increased corner speed. It's more "modern" to use less steering lock than in previous years.
- Hole in shock cap drilled to approximately 1mm (front and rear) to achieve minimum rebound.
- Steering system — shim under ball cup reduced from 1mm to 0.5mm for less aggressive initial steering.
- Front suspension arms moved rearwards by increasing hinge pin shim at front from 1mm to 1.25mm and reducing spacer at rear from 1.5mm to 1mm. This is a personal preference only.
- Front suspension blocks FF from A3 in to A3 out, and FR from A3 in to A3 out. This increases the track width (approximately 190mm) which is usually better for carpet. The alternative when increasing track width would be to use a wider wheel hex, but this does not feel as good/well balanced.
- Rear suspension blocks RF as kit setup (NA3 in), but RR from A3 out to A3 in reducing the rear track width to approximately 188mm. The car works best with a track width split of around 2mm front-to-rear.
- Front camber link ball stud shims reduced (inner from 1.5mm to 0.5mm and outer from 2mm to 1.5mm). I carried this over from my BD9 setup.
- Rear camber link ball stud shims changed (inner from 0.5mm to 0mm and outer from 1mm to 1.25mm). I carried this over from my BD9 setup.
- Front shock tower damper upper position changed from outside to mid hole (laying shocks down by one position).
- Thicker shock oil from 350 cSt to Axon 35 Wt (which is approximately 450–500 cSt).
- Centre Stiffness:
    - Cross Centre Post — no screws from top deck. These screws should only be installed in high traction to stiffen the car. On a track like Longwy, it would reduce steering in the corner.

- - Did not install Rear Carbon Stiffener as it would make car too stiff for this track.
- T-plate upside down, making it flat on the chassis.
- Rear hub carrier standard rather than graphite. Personal preference.
- Rear toe-in from 3.8° to 2.7°. This is my normal starting setting.
- I was using a shorty battery, so with the brass holder in front and back of the battery (40g each), I needed another 35g under the battery to maintain balance. A further 35g under the receiver was added to achieve the needed 1320g and to keep 50/50 front/rear weight bias (which is best for the BD10 on carpet).

Body, radio, motor and ESC settings:

- Xtreme Twister body and wing. This was the best choice of body shell for the 2019/2020 winter season and 2020 summer season. It had the most grip and steering, but the rear is not stuck or planted and remains "free".
- Throttle and Brake EPA both 96%.
- Throttle Expo -15% (Sanwa). Brake Expo not used.
- LRP X22 5.0t motor with 19.5° of timing and a 12.1mm rotor.
- Final Drive Ratio 7.892.
- LRP X TC Spec V4.3 ESC:
  - Drag Brake: 9%.
  - Brake Type: BDX20.
  - Initial Brake: 18%.
  - Initial Drive: 1%.
  - Torque Feel: 5 (out of 10).
  - Timing: 20°.
  - Ramp: 7°/10kRPM.
  - Delay: 25kRPM.
  - Trigger Dependency: 3 (out of 10).
  - Automatic Turbo: Off.
- **Tyre Treatment** — MR33 V4 additive applied for 10 minutes across the entire surface of the front and rear tyres. Tyre warmers were not used.

2nd — Marc Rheinard — Awesomatix A800MMX

This was my first race meeting with the Awesomatix. I made changes for every run. I could feel the impact of every little change on the car. I'd never had this before, and I really liked it! This was my final setup:

- Ride height 5.2mm front, 5.4mm rear.
- Front droop 5.7mm, rear 4.6mm.
- Front toe-out 1°.
- Front and rear camber -2°.
- Caster front 5° and rear 2°.
- Front and rear dampers 400 cSt.
- Diff oil 10,000 cSt.
- Diff height low.
- Xtreme Twister 0.5 body.
- **Tyre Treatment** — Additive applied for 10 minutes across the entire surface of the front and rear tyres. Tyre warmers were not used.

Valentin Hettrich and Olivier Bultynck also ran the Awesomatix in the Stock class. You can see their setup later in this section and compare it to Marc's setup above.

Continuing with Marc's final setup:

- Shorty lipo.
- 1326g race ready weight with 48% front and 52% rear weight distribution.
- Final Drive Ratio 7.33.
- Muchmore Fleta ZX V2 5.0T HE motor with 20 degrees of timing.

ESC setup (Muchmore Fleta):

- 10% drag brake.
- Initial Brake=drag brake.
- 95% full brake, 1.3Hz, linear.
- Power level (0–30): 20.
- BT Soft Power (0–20): 10.
- BT Soft TH Range (0–75%): 50%.
- Drive Frequency: 22KHz.
- Neutral Dead Band (0–12%): 6%.
- Boost Timing (0–60°): 0.
- Turbo:
    - Turbo Timing (0–60°): 28.
    - On Slope: Instant.
    - Off Slope: Instant.
    - Delay: 0.1 sec.

8th – Alexander Hagberg – Xray T4'20

The following settings were left as per the manufacturer's kit setup:

- Front ride height 5.2mm.
- Droop front 5.6mm, rear 4.6mm.
- Camber front and rear -2°.
- Caster front 4°.
- Chassis aluminium-flex.
- Diff position front and rear are up.
- Shock oil 450 cSt front and rear.
- Roll bars front 1.4mm and rear 1.3mm.

Alexander's normal carpet setup is different to the manufacturer's basic carpet setup as follows:

- Gear diff oil increased from 5,000 to 8,000 cSt.
- Front springs from 2.5 to progressive 2.5–2.8.
- Rear springs from 2.5 to 2.6.
- Suspension arm mount Rear Front (RF) changed from Std to 0.25.
- Roll Centre — Front FF to outside-mid 0.5.
- Roll Centre — Rear RF to outside-top 0.5 and RR to mid-top 0.5.
- Rear ride height dropped to 5.2mm.
- Rear toe-in reduced from 3mm to 2.25mm.
- Front toe-out from 1mm to 1.25mm.
- Ackermann shim reduced from 1mm to 0mm.
- Steering plate reduced from 8.5mm to 8mm.
- Changed driveshafts from 51mm to 52mm.
- Steering lock from 26° to 25°.
- Shorty lipo using optional battery holders #306195.
- Track Width narrower front and rear by 0.75mm.

Alexander explains each of these changes as follows:

Diff oil — The 8000 cSt (fairly heavy) rear diff oil is typical for medium to high grip carpet racing, compared to the 5000 cSt, which is the basic setup. A heaver diff oil makes the car turn more on-power and improves forward traction (if the track grip allows for it). 8000 was a setting I used for most indoor events over the last carpet season, especially when Volante control tyres were used.

Springs — Compared to the linear 2.5 kit springs, the progressive 2.5–2.8 front spring, in combination with the linear 2.6 rear spring, not only sharpens the steering response but also improves cornering speed. This is my basic setting for 90% of all carpet tracks and is also a good basic setting for asphalt. The kit springs are rather soft, which makes the car nice and forgiving to drive, but not as fast as with the stiffer/progressive springs.

Arm Sweep — The front arm sweep has been changed using the FF roll centre inserts in the 0.5 outer position. This introduces "arm sweep" or "inboard toe-out" into the suspension, which means that the FF inserts are wider than the FR inserts (which are centred). This gives the car better initial steering, as it gives a slight reactive caster effect on suspension compression.

Bump steer — The bump steer effect has been increased from the kit setup, by adding a 0.5mm shim under the steering block. This makes the car more aggressive, since it gives it more steering, mainly in the middle of the corner.

Roll centre (rear – suspension arms) — The rear roll centre has not only been raised, by using both the RF and RR inserts 0.5 higher, but the RF is also wider than the RR, which reduced the overall toe-in of the car. The higher rear roll centre makes the rear end of the car flatter (less chassis roll) which helps the car to stay more consistent, mainly on quick direction changes, such as chicanes, which is beneficial for medium to high grip carpet racing. The toe-in has been reduced to help the car to turn better in tight corners.

Roll centre (rear – camber links) — The rear roll centre has been lowered by raising the camber link on the rear inside point from 1 to 1.5mm. This roll centre change makes the car more aggressive (more rotation).

> *About the rear roll centre:* The two roll centre changes (above) are doing slightly different things. The suspension arm position affects mainly the way the car rolls. But changing the camber link height also affects the camber gain (camber change) when the car rolls. In this case, raising the inner point of the camber link will both lower the roll centre, but at the same time, decrease the camber gain on suspension compression. This combination of settings seemed to be the exactly right ones for these particular conditions.

Ackermann — The Ackermann angle has been increased from the kit setup by using no shims, instead of the suggested 1mm. This will give the car a bit less initial steering, but will "free up" the car for higher grip conditions.

Steering plate — The kit 8.5mm Ackermann plate was replaced by an optional 8.0mm plate. This Ackermann change helps the car to carry better cornering speed and isn't as twitchy initially. Mainly recommended for higher grip conditions.

Steering arms — I was using the optional #302525 aluminium steering arms, which gives the car better response compared to the kit plastic arms.

Steering shim — The steering lock has been physically limited by the use of a larger diameter shim at the centre of the steering (7.5mm instead of 6.0mm, which comes with the kit). Less steering lock makes the car less twitchy and increases cornering speeds.

Servo horn — The kit servo saver has been replaced by a direct servo horn, which gives the car a more direct steering feel, which is recommended for top level competition.

Top deck — The kit 2.0mm top deck was replaced with the 1.6mm optional top deck, for more flexibility. This makes the car turn better, as it allows the car to flex more, especially at the middle of the corner.

Top deck flex — The standard setting is a bushing fitted at the rear of the topdeck (less flexible). I opted for the bearing option, which allows the topdeck to flex more from side-to-side, which increases rotation. Recommended for Modified racing, especially.

Motor mount flex — I removed two screws from my motor mount, one in front and one behind the spur gear, to increase flexibility. This gives the car more grip, especially on-power. This setting has been much preferred by the team over the kit "full stiff" setting.

Chassis Brace — I was also using the optional rear T-brace, which stiffens up the rear of the chassis. This increases stability and decreases rotation. Mainly recommended for medium to high grip carpet racing — to make the car more predictable.

Drive shaft — The kit front 51mm driveshafts were swapped to the 52mm ones. The longer driveshaft makes the car smoother (less initial steering) but helps the car to finish the corner better (turns more from the middle to the exit of the corner).

Track Width — The kit offset hexes have been swapped to optional -0.75mm ones, to make the car narrower. The narrower track width allows the car to turn in harder, and to change direction faster. Mainly recommended for Modified racing.

Motor — Hobbywing G3 5.0T motor with 35 degrees of timing. I use a 5.0T motor for indoor carpet racing, because of the track sizes being smaller and more twisty in general. Outdoors, where tracks are bigger and with longer straights, I usually choose a 4.5T motor of the same type.

All the above changes are really not specific for GP3F in Longwy, but are very general changes that I also made for other indoor events throughout the carpet season, such as the first and second round of the ETS series, in Vienna, Austria, and Daun, Germany respectively. My car setup over these three events changed very little. It came down to fine-tuning!

Event Specific Changes

- **ESC Settings** — I find an FDR of 7.46 is very well suited for most carpet tracks and doesn't need to be changed. However, we do tend to play with the ESC settings to fine-tune the feel for different tracks (rather than gear ratio). For example, on a bigger track, we may add boost and turbo. And for a smaller track, we reduce those parameters. I also set different drag brake depending on grip levels. Tracks with higher grip and more tight turns usually require a higher drag brake setting to help the car turn.

  My ESC boost and turbo settings for this particular race were 3 and 28. My drag brake was set at 14%.

- **Body** — Extreme Twister 0.5mm body shell with Twister 0.7mm wing.

  One thing which was specific for the GP3F event in Longwy was the use of a lightweight bodyshell (0.5mm instead of 0.75mm) because the race regulation had no limit for the bodyshell weight (unlike the ETS).

- **Top Deck** — I also ran a narrower top deck, which in fact, was a prototype part, and is now a production part for the soon to be released T4'21 chassis. This is proof that myself and the rest of the factory team are constantly developing and changing our platform, also in preparation for the release of a new version of the chassis that following year.

- **Tyre Treatment** — I cleaned the tyres with additive before applying additive for the next race. 10 minutes before the race, I treated the entire surface of all four tyres with additive and let it air dry. I didn't use tyre warmers.

I tested different additives throughout the weekend, since there was no spec additive for this race. I tested both CS High Grip (a typical oil-based carpet additive) and MR33 V4 which is the spec additive for the ETS series. Both gave a similar performance, but with the MR33 V4 proving to be more consistent.

Jan Ratheisky also ran the Xray, in the Stock class. You can see his setup below and compare it to Alexander's setup above.

Stock (13.5T Motor)

The top 10 from the 120 entries in the Stock Class:

1st Jan Ratheisky (Xray), 2nd Valentin Hettrich (Awesomatix), 3rd Olivier Bultynck (Awesomatix), 4th Leo Arnold (Xray), 5th Frederick Mikkelsen (Awesomatix), 6th Nicolas Delisé (Awesomatix), 7th Hannes Soyke, 8th Kevin Nielsen (Xray), 9th Tobias Vogel (Awesomatix), 10th Tim Benson (Xray)

1st (and TQ) — Jan Ratheisky — Xray T4'20

Jan's carpet setup compared to the manufacturer's basic carpet setup as follows:

- Gear diff oil increased from 5,000 to 8,000 cSt.
- Front springs from 2.5 to progressive 2.5–2.8.
- Rear springs from 2.5 to 2.6.
- Roll Centre — Front FF to outside-mid 1.0.
- Roll Centre — Rear RF to outside-mid 0.5.
- Rear ride height dropped to 5.2mm.
- Rear toe-in reduced from 3mm to 2.5mm.
- Ackermann shim reduced from 1mm to 0.5mm.
- Steering plate reduced from 8.5mm to 8mm.
- Suspension arm mount Rear Front (RF) changed from Std to 0.25.
- Changed rear driveshafts from 51mm CVD to 52mm ECS.

- Changed rear suspension arms from long to short.
- Lay down front and rear shocks from position 2 (mid) to position 1 (inner).
- Changed standard shock towers to low shock towers.

Changes made for this event:

- Hobbywing 13.5 motor with 54° timing.
- FDR 4.75 to obtain acceleration out of the many slow corners.
- **Tyre Treatment** — Additive applied for 8 minutes across the entire surface of the front and rear tyres. Tyre warmers were not used.

Changes during qualifying:

- **After Q1** — raised inner camber link for a looser rear and more steering.
- **After Q2** — changed low shock towers to normal shock towers to increase car roll and provide more grip.
- **After Q3** — reduced top deck thickness from 2mm to 1.6mm for greater flex and traction. Reduced rear toe-in from 2.5mm to 2.25mm for a rear that rotates more easily.

2ⁿᵈ — Valentin Hettrich — Awesomatix A800MMX

- Ride height 5.2mm front, 5.4mm rear.
- Front droop 5.8mm, rear 4.8mm.
- Front and rear camber -2°.
- Caster 5°.
- Front toe-out 1°, rear toe-in 2.25°.
- Front and rear dampers 400cSt.
- Diff oil 10,000cSt.
- Bittydesign Hyper body. Because of my driving style I like calm and precise cars and this body provides that.
- 1321g race ready weight with 49% front and 51% rear weight distribution.
- Final Drive Ratio 4.75. In my opinion this is the best ratio for a track like Longwy, because of its size. If you use a lower ratio, then perhaps you have a slightly faster car at the end of the straight, but the effect is minimal and not noticeable in a fight. But 4.75 is better on run time, temperature and motor efficiency.

I was happy with my car from the start of this event, the only issue was the rear was a little loose. I tried the following to fix this:

1. **Upper roll centre** — lowered the rear roll centre. This made no noticeable difference to traction, but reduced corner speed, so I put it back the way it was.
2. **Top deck screws** — I started with 2 of the 3 rear top deck screws in place (screws D and E). I tried removing screw E. This made no noticeable difference, and I put it back.
3. **Motor mount flex setting** — the Awesomatix has five screws from under the chassis into the motor mount. Using screws 1, 2 and 3 (only) make the car more agile in the middle of the corner (this was my starting point). I removed screw 1. The car felt better, but having only 2 screws holding the motor mount meant the car was tweaked after every run. So, I removed screw 2 and added screws 4 and 5. Using screws 3, 4 and 5 (only) made the car easier to drive with slight understeer, without the tweak issues. I kept this setting. This change made the car more stable and much easier to drive flawlessly over the 5 minutes. At this point, I was very happy with the car.

Tyre Treatment — I cleaned the tyres with brake cleaner after each run. Then, 15 minutes before the race, I treated the entire surface of all four tyres with additive and let it air dry. After 6 minutes, I did it again. The tyres were dry when I put the car on the track without needing to wipe them. I didn't use tyre warmers.

3rd — Olivier Bultynck — Awesomatix A800MMX

- Ride height 5.2mm front, 5.4mm rear.
- Front droop 5.8mm, rear 4.6mm.
- Front and rear camber -2°.
- Caster 4°.
- Front and rear dampers 400cSt.
- Diff oil 8,000cSt.
- Xtreme Twister 0.7 body.
- Final Drive Ratio 4.32.

Tyre Treatment — About 20 minutes before the race I treated the entire surface of all tyres with additive and let it air dry. After 8 minutes I did it again. I didn't use tyre warmers.

Asphalt Case Studies

Starting Setup

If you have not raced at a particular track before, we recommend starting with your chassis manufacturer's base asphalt setup. You may also wish to search your chassis manufacturer's website for another driver's setup at that track so you can note the changes they made. We do not recommend using another driver's setup without knowing why they made the changes they did. However, it can be very useful to note the differences to the manufacturer's base asphalt setup and then try each change, one at a time, and note whether it feels better or worse.

Changes Compared to Carpet

1. Asphalt tracks tend to be bumpier than carpet and therefore you should use a higher ride height.
2. Asphalt generally provides less grip than a carpet track. Therefore, the car will normally be less stiff in order to provide sufficient grip.
3. Tyre wear on asphalt is significantly greater than on carpet.
4. Asphalt tracks are normally outdoors and therefore track temperatures will change throughout the day.

Case Study Track

Euro Touring Series (ETS) Round 3, Arena 33, Andernach, Germany. Medium-high grip asphalt. Mixed track with both fast and technical sections. Medium-large size track. This event was held during the Covid-19 pandemic with appropriate social distance and mask wearing.

Case Studies 8

Track Temperature
15–45°C (59–113°F).

Control Tyre
Volante V8 36R.

Control Additive
MR33 V3 Asphalt.

Special thanks to Euro Touring Series and rc-car-pics.de for the ETS Round 3 photos.

190

Modified

1st Ronald Völker (Yokomo), 2nd Marc Rheinard (Awesomatix), 3rd Lucas Urbain (Awesomatix), 4th Bruno Coelho (Xray), 5th Alexander Hagberg (Xray), 6th Michal Orlowski (Schumacher), 7th Yannic Prümper (Awesomatix), 8th Christopher Krapp (Yokomo), 9th Antoine Brunet (Awesomatix), 10th Marco Kaufmann (Xray), 11th Viktor Wilck (Infinity)

In Qualifying:

- Ronald Völker (Yokomo) won Q1 ahead of Lucas Urbain (Awesomatix) and Bruno Coelho (Xray).
- In Q2 Ronald won with second and third places reversed from Q1.
- Marc Rheinard (Awesomatix) took the win in Q3 followed by Völker and Coelho.
- Q4 would decide pole position between German rivals Rheinard and Völker, but Lucas Urbain took his first ever ETS qualifying round win, Rheinard second and Alexander Hagberg (Xray) third.

The final lineup was Völker as top qualifier on pole position ahead of Rheinard, Urbain, Coelho and Hagberg.

In the finals, A1 saw a battle between Völker and Rheinard. These two built a small gap and left Urbain and Coelho fighting for third. Rheinard kept the pressure on Völker, but with ninety seconds to go, Rheinard began to drop back and Völker took the win. The top four finished in grid order with Yannic Prumper (Awesomatix) taking fifth, up from ninth on the grid.

A2 saw Rheinard right on Völker's bumper with Urbain sticking with the German drivers and looking like he could challenge Rheinard. However, sixty seconds into the race, the Frenchman rolled, ending his challenge. Although Rheinard kept up the pressure, Völker made no errors and took A2 and the overall event win. Coelho third and Hagberg fourth, the two Xray drivers finishing about 1.5 seconds behind the leaders. Michal Orlowski (Schumacher) took fifth.

With Völker having sealed the win in A2, A3 would decide the rest of the podium. Drivers were even on pace, none able to pass, and the cars circulated in grid order. Rheinard took A2, securing second overall, ahead of Urbain, who would take the last step on the podium.

TQ & 1st — Ronald Völker — Yokomo BD10

The following settings were changed when compared to Ronald's GP3F carpet setup (above):

- Carbon fibre chassis.
- Chassis stiffness — flex increased by removing front two screws and T-plate removed. Centre post connected with screw and 1mm shim to top deck. This is a normal change when moving to a carbon fibre chassis on asphalt.
- Front ride height from 5.1mm to 5.0mm. Rear ride height increased from 5.3mm to 5.5mm. This achieved a split of 0.5mm. I'd set up a fairly soft rear and with less than 5.5mm in the rear it would touch the ground too often.
- Front sway bar decreased from 1.4mm to 1.3mm.
- Used Active Rear Suspension (ARS).
- Front droop reduced from 6mm to 5.8mm (front edge) and rear droop 4.8mm (rear edge) which is roughly equivalent to 2.3mm (centre side).

- Steering lock from 25° to 24°. Provides increased corner speed. I try to use as little lock as possible to maintain corner speed, without compromising steering too much.
- Front shock spring from 2.4–2.9 progressive to 2.5–2.8 progressive. 2.4–2.9 in front has less roll, so it's better for carpet, but not for asphalt.
- Rear shock spring from 2.45–2.75 progressive to 2.3–3.0 progressive. Rear shock oil increased from Axon 35Wt (which is approximately 450–500 cSt) to 37.5Wt. I use ARS outdoors and it has quite a different geometry, so usually ARS setup requires harder shock setup due to more weight. It's therefore a matter of using the right combination of oil, spring and shock position.
- Steering system — shim under ball cup reduced from 0.5mm to 0mm for less aggressive initial steering.
- Rear toe-in increased from 2.7° to 3°.
- Diff oil was a half and half mix of 5,000 and 7,500 cSt to achieve a viscosity approximately in the middle (I didn't have a 6,000 cSt oil handy). 5K was a little "too free" during the run and 7.5K felt off balance.
- Rear shocks laid down from the outside position to the centre position on the tower.
- Front roll centre changed by increasing the inner camber link shim from 0.5mm to 1.5mm.
- Rear roll centre changed by increasing inner camber link shims from 0mm to 1.5mm and outer camber link shims from 1.25mm to 1.5mm.
- Front suspension arm FF spacer from 1.5mm to 2.3mm and FR from 1.5mm to 2.5mm, raising the front roll centre.
- Rear suspension arm RF spacer from 1.5mm to 2.8mm and FR from 1.5mm to 2.8mm. Rear suspension blocks not changed. ARS has different arm length and straight arms, so the toe-in comes from the hub sides. In general, higher roll centre feels like more grip and side bite, but also greater understeer.
- Reduced front track width by reducing front wheel hex spacer from 1mm to 0.25mm. Theoretically this provides more steering, but basically I like to keep front-to-rear track width within 2mm of a difference (with the front being wider).
- Reduced rear track width by reducing rear wheel hex spacer from 1mm to 0mm. The ARS system gives a different track width to normal.

- Front suspension FF block from A3 out to 2 out. FR also from A3 out to 2 out, narrowing the car by 0.4mm
- Diff position front and rear unchanged (high).
- Shock travel — front shock shaft gap 7.7mm and rear 8mm.
- I used a full size battery as a shorty battery wouldn't make the 5 minute race run time.

Body, radio, motor and ESC settings:

- Xtreme Twister 0.7 body and wing. This was the best choice of body shell for the 2019/2020 winter season and 2020 summer season. It had the most grip and steering, but the rear is not stuck or planted and remains "free".
- Throttle EPA 95% and Brake EPA 92%.
- Throttle Expo -9% (Sanwa). Brake Expo not used.
- LRP X22 5.0t motor with 17° of timing and a 12.3mm rotor (rather than the 12.1mm).
- Final Drive Ratio 7.32.
- LRP X TC Spec V4.3 ESC:
    - Drag Brake: 3% (down from 9% on carpet) to provide more corner speed.
    - Brake Type: BDX20.
    - Initial Brake: 18%.
    - Initial Drive: 1%.
    - Torque Feel: 3 (out of 10). (Down from 5).
    - Timing: 36° (up from 20°).
    - Ramp: 11°/10kRPM.
    - Delay: 15kRPM.
    - Trigger Dependency: 2 (out of 10).
    - Automatic Turbo: On (instead of Off).
- **Tyre Treatment** — additive applied across the entire surface of the front and rear tyres. Tyre warmers used for 15 minutes at 65–70°C (149–158°F).

2nd — Marc Rheinard — Awesomatix A800MMX

This was my final setup. I've noted changes from my carpet setup at the GP3F race:

- Changed from the Aluminium chassis used at GP3F to the carbon fibre chassis, for added flex.
- Roll centre — I lowered the front roll centre as follows:
    - Front suspension arm shims increased from 1.75mm to 2mm.
    - Front inner camber link shims decreased from 3.75mm to 3.5mm.
- Rear shock and shock spring made harder by changing from 98.2 GF/MM to 108.4 GF/MM and the sliding screw next to it from 1.6mm to 3mm (on an Awesomatix the higher the numbers the harder it is). On another brand of car, the equivalent would be to change the shock position and the springs.
- Front and rear dampers 400 cSt.
- Ride height 5.0mm front, 5.4mm rear. Front ride height reduced 0.2mm compared to GP3F.
- Front droop 5.6mm, rear 4.6mm.
- Front toe-out 1°.
- Rear toe-in 3°. Increased from 2.5°.
- Front and rear camber -2°.
- Caster front 4° and rear 4°. Front caster decreased from 5°, rear increased from 2°.
- Diff oil 7,000 cSt. Reduced from 10,000.
- Diff height high. Changed from low.
- Xtreme Twister 0.7 body. Increased thickness from 0.5. The ETS series has body weight rules.
- **Tyre Treatment** — Additive applied for 15 minutes across the entire surface of the front and rear tyres. I didn't use tyre warmers.

Continuing with Marc's final setup:

- Shorty lipo.
- Final Drive Ratio 7.34.

- Muchmore Fleta ZX V2 4.5T motor with 20 degrees of timing (standard for this motor). The 4.5T suited this track size and layout.

ESC setup (Muchmore Fleta) — I used the same settings as I did at GP3F, except for Turbo :
- 10% drag brake.
- Initial Brake=drag brake.
- 95% full brake, 1.3Hz, linear.
- Power level (0–30): 20.
- BT Soft Power (0–20): 10.
- BT Soft TH Range (0–75%): 50%.
- Drive Frequency: 22KHz.
- Neutral Dead Band (0–12%): 6%.
- Boost Timing (0–60°): 0.
- Turbo:
    - Turbo Timing (0–60°): 20 (down from 28 at GP3F). This setting suited the track size and layout.
    - On Slope: Instant.
    - Off Slope: Instant.
    - Delay: 0.1 sec.

5th — Alexander Hagberg — Xray T4 '20

Below is Alexander's final setup. The following were unchanged from his carpet setup on page *179*:

- Front ride height 5.2mm. Rear 5.2mm.
- Camber front and rear -2°.
- Caster front 4°.
- Front toe-out 1.25mm.
- Diff position front and rear is up.
- Front springs progressive 2.5–2.8.

- Shock oil 450 cSt front and rear.
- Suspension arm mount Rear Front (RF) 0.25.
- Roll Centre — Front FF outside-mid 0.5.
- Ackermann shim 0mm.
- Steering plate 8mm.
- Driveshafts 52mm.
- Roll bar rear 1.3mm.

Changes made from his carpet setup (on page *179*) were as follows:

- Chassis graphite (changed from aluminium-flex).
- Track Width wider by changing the -0.75mm wheel hexes back to the standard ones.
- Droop front 5.6mm, rear 4.4mm (rear lowered by 0.2mm compared to carpet).
- Gear diff oil reduced from 8,000 to 7,000 cSt. Arena 33 has good grip for an asphalt track but still less than carpet.
- Roll bar front 1.4mm to 1.3mm.
- Rear springs from 2.6 to 2.7.
- Rear toe-in increased from 2.25mm to 2.5mm.
- Active Rear Suspension used with toe-gain with very little inboard toe-in, to try and free up the rear.
- Roll Centre — Rear RF to outside-top from 0.5 to 1.0 and RR to mid-top from 0.5 to 1.0 raising the rear roll centre. This is very high for the suspension arms, again to try and free up the rear.
- Steering lock from 25° to 28° to help the car turn in better in the tight corners.
- Motor Hobbywing G3 4.5T with 35° of end bell timing and 12.1mm rotor.
- Final Drive Ratio 7.4.
- ESC Settings (Hobbywing XERUN XR10 Pro G2):
    - Throttle Rate: 20 (options are from 1–30)
    - Throttle Curve: Linear
    - Coast: 0% (0–20%)

- Drive Frequency: 8K (1K–32K)
- Softening Value: 20° (0–30)
- Softening Range: 30% (0–75%)
- Drag Brake: 14%
- Brake Force: 100%
- Initial Brake = Drag Brake
- Brake Rate Control: 20 (1–20), Frequency 1K (1K–16K)
- Brake Curve and Brake Control both Linear.
- Boost: 8° Start RPM: 7,500, End RPM: 22,500
- Turbo Timing: 36° Delay: 0.1 sec
- Turbo Increase Rate: 18°/0.1 sec
- Turbo Decrease Rate: Instant. This is because of the hard braking point and 180° corner at the end of the straight. Running instant turbo decrease helps the car to slow down faster.

- **Tyre Treatment** — Cleaned tyres with brake cleaner before applying additive. Additive applied for 15 minutes across the entire surface of the front and rear tyres. Tyres warmers set to 65°C (149°F).

Stock (13.5T Motor)

1st Alexandre Duchet (Xray), 2nd Simon Lauter (Awesomatix), 3rd Max Mächler (Awesomatix), 4th Kevin Nielsen (Xray), 5th Casper Lund (Awesomatix), 6th Lukas Ellerbrock (Xray), 7th Fabian Bucher (Awesomatix), 8th Frederik Mikkelsen (Awesomatix), 9th Alex Kunkler (Yokomo), 10th Tim Benson (Xray), 11th Lars Hoppe (ARC)

In the Stock (Pro Stock) class, ETS specifies:

- A handout 13.5T motor with fixed end bell timing.
- A handout ESC (non-timing/blinky mode) with motor RPM limited to 25,000.
- Final Drive Ratio may be no lower than 4.5 for asphalt races.

In Qualifying:

- Frederik Mikkelsen (Awesomatix) took Q1, ahead of fellow Danish driver Kevin Nielsen (Xray).
- Q2 saw Simon Lauter (Awesomatix) take control, beating out Alexandre Duchet (Xray).
- Q3 went to Max Mächler (Awesomatix), with Lauter in second place.
- In Q4 Duchet took the win with Nielsen in second.

Case Studies 8

Four different winners showed just how tight the competition was for top qualifier. After tie breaks, Duchet secured pole position ahead of Lauter, Mikkelsen, Mächler and Nielsen.

In the finals, Lauter battled with teammate Mächler for second place and came out ahead. At the front, Alexandre Duchet took the win in A1.

In A2 Lauter nipped at the heels of Duchet, but couldn't deny the French driver the win. With wins in A1 and A2 Duchet took the overall win. Lauter took the win in A3 to confirm second overall, with Mächler rounding out the overall podium.

TQ & 1st — Alexandre Duchet — Xray T4 '20

During the meeting we changed the car to find more steering because the track is very technical with a lot of direction changes. Then we worked to maximise the new V8 tyres. For the changes on the car we changed: Ackermann, the front roll bar, the front position of the steering servo (moved forward using optional part) and the roll centre front and rear. With all these changes, and the help of Martin Hudy, it allowed me to have a fast and consistent car during all qualifiers and finals.

Final setup (compared to kit asphalt setup) was:

- Ride height front 5mm, rear 5.2mm.
- Droop front 5.6mm, rear 4.6mm.
- Front toe-out 1°.
- Rear toe-in 2.5°.
- Front and rear camber -2°.
- Ackermann shim reduced from 1mm to 0mm.

- Roll bar front changed from 1.4mm to 1.3mm, rear 1.3mm (unchanged).
- Steering lock 28°.
- Front springs from 2.5 to progressive 2.5–2.8.
- Rear springs from 2.5 to 2.6.
- Shock oil 450 cSt with 0% rebound.
- Changed front driveshafts from 51mm CVD to 52mm ECS.
- Roll Centre & Arm Sweep set at the suspension blocks:
    - Front FF to outside-mid 0.5mm. Roll centre unchanged. Arm sweep added.
    - Rear RF to outside-top 0.5mm. Rear RR to mid-top 0.5mm. Rear roll centre higher. Arm sweep added.
- Diff height high.
- Gear diff oil increased from 5,000 to 7,000 cSt.
- Altered chassis flex by changing screws under the chassis as follows: moved 2 screws from standard to forward position, removed screw either side of motor mount, removed rear chassis brace.
- Final Drive Ratio 4.51.
- Xtreme Twister body.
- **Tyre Treatment** — Additive applied for 15 minutes across the entire surface of the front and rear tyres. Tyre warmers were used.

2nd – Simon Lauter – Awesomatix A800MMX

Final setup:

- Ride height 4.8mm front, 5.2mm rear.
- Droop front 5.6mm, rear 4.2mm.
- Front toe-out 1°.
- Rear toe-in 2.5°.
- Front and rear camber -2.5°.
- Caster front 5° and rear 3°.
- Ackermann position front.

- Roll Bars front 1.2mm, rear 1.1mm.
- Steering lock 25°.
- Front and rear dampers Axon 37.5 Wt. I used thinner shock oil when the track was cold to generate more grip and thicker oil as the temperature came up.
- Diff height high.
- Xtreme Twister body.
- Weight 1321g with weight distribution of 49.5% front, 50.5% rear.
- Final Drive Ratio 4.51.
- **Tyre Treatment** — Additive applied for 20 minutes across the entire surface of the front and rear tyres and then applied again for a further 10 minutes. Tyre warmers were set to 60–65°C (140–149°F).

Initially, the car understeered on this track quite badly. Changes made to overcome this were:

- Diff oil 7,500 cSt for more on-power steering.
- Increased flex by changing the motor mount and top deck screws/locations.
- Roll centre front was raised by increasing shims under the front suspension arms by 0.5mm. This helped a great deal as it made the car more precise.

3rd — Max Mächler — Awesomatix A800MMX

- Ride height 4.8mm front, 5.2mm rear.
- Droop front 5.6mm, rear 4.4mm.
- Front toe-out 1.2°.
- Anti-dive using 0.5mm shim under rear of front suspension arm. I usually run anti-dive as it generates more steering in slower parts of the track, and this gives me more freedom on the steering wheel for corrections.
- Rear toe-in 2.5°.
- Front and rear camber -2.5°.
- Caster front 5° and rear 3°.
- Ackermann position max forward.
- Roll Bars front 1.2mm, rear 1.1mm.
- Steering lock 25°.
- Front and rear dampers Axon 50 Wt.
- Diff oil 10,000 cSt.
- Diff height high.
- Xtreme Twister body.

- Weight 1325g with weight distribution of 49% front, 51% rear.
- Final Drive Ratio 4.51.
- **Tyre Treatment** — Additive applied for 15 minutes across the entire surface of the front and rear tyres. Tyre warmers were set to 65°C (149°F).

Front Roll Centre — Higher

By increasing shims under the front suspension arms by 0.5mm.

Reason: The balance between front and rear traction was not perfect for the current conditions. The car had too much steering for the first 2–3 laps, causing the tyres to overheat. This then required more steering lock, which reduced corner speed. By raising the front roll centre, my goal was to reduce tyre heat and keep the front tyres in the working range.

Result on track: Success. The tyres didn't overheat and needed less steering lock to make the corners, which means more corner speed. Overall balance felt great!

Front Toe-out

Changed from 1.0° per side to 1.2° per side.

Reason: The car was very nervous with the new Volante V8 tyres down the back straight and a bit too nimble into the chicane/front of drivers stand. By setting slightly more toe-out, it was my goal to calm down the car in these areas. More front toe generated a bit more drag, but at the same time generated more "leading force" for the tyres.

Result on track: It was exactly what I was looking for. Car was easier to drive, which allowed me to drive it more consistently. Please keep in mind that 0.2° is a very small change.

Gear Diff Oil

Increased from 7,500 cSt to 10,000 cSt oil in the gear diff.

Reason: I noted my lap times dropped a bit at the end of the run. I wanted more consistency for the full 5 minute race.

Result on track: The drop off for the last 2 minutes of the race was less. However, I needed to heat the diff before the start of the race, otherwise the first minute was too hard to drive out of the corners on throttle. Heating was achieved by holding the right rear tyre while squeezing the throttle gently for 20–30 seconds.

Rear Bump Steer

Added 1mm shim.

Reason: The car didn't change direction quickly in tight corners and in the chicane. I wanted to free up the rear end as it was reducing corner speed.

Result on track: Gained more rotation and more corner speed. Rear end grip was still good enough.

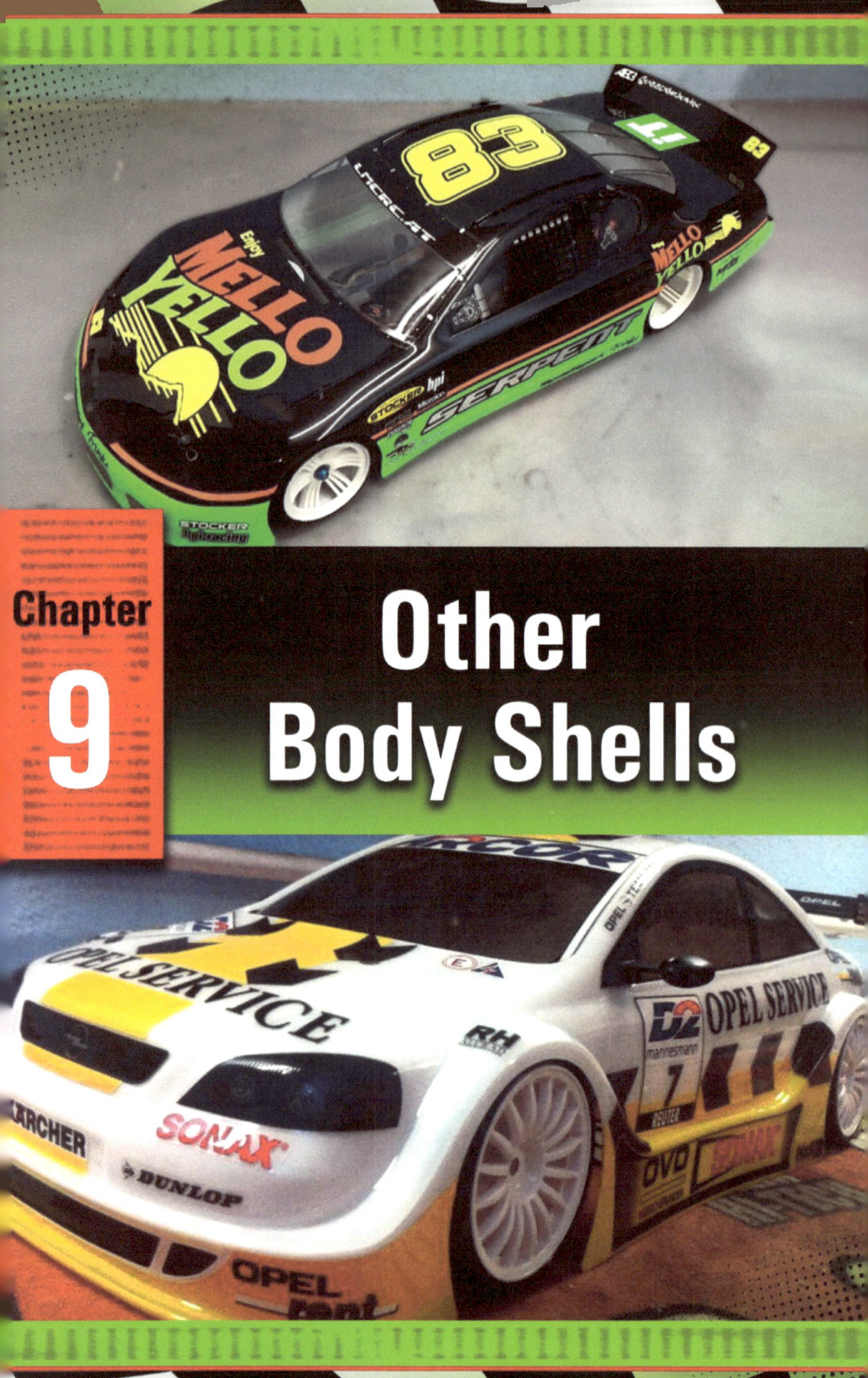

Chapter 9

Other Body Shells

Other Body Shells 9

[Previous page — Top: NASCAR livery used in the movie Days of Thunder. Bottom: Opel Astra DTM]

Competitive RC Touring Car shells are designed to maximise aerodynamics and provide the fastest lap times possible. You can see those types of body shells used throughout this book. However, this chapter showcases the scale realism which is also an enjoyable part of the hobby.

Touring Cars

These shells are probably legal to run in most classes (check your local rules). They are often used for drifting or as display bodies:

Mercedes C Class DTM

Ford Mustang

Opel Calibra

Subaru Impreza

BMW E92 M3 DTM

Other Body Shells

Opel Calibra

Audi R8

BMW E90
3 Series

BMW E30 M3

Nissan R35 GTR GT1

Opel Astra DTM

Other Body Shells 9

Vintage Trans Am

Vintage Trans Am (or Vintage Touring Car) are normally American muscle cars with body shells from the late 1960s to early 1970s. They often race with control tyres (check your local rules):

Pontiac Trans Am

1970 Ford Mustang

1966 Ford Mustang

Ford Mustang (left) and 1970 Plymouth Cuda (right)

1968 Ford Mustang

1970 Ford Mustang Boss 302

Other Body Shells 9

GT

The GT class normally runs any 2-door GT (Grand Touring) shell (check your local rules):

Chevy Camaro ZL1 (above and below)

Mercedes SLS GT3 2012 — Ferrari 458 GT3

Ford GT 2016

Ford Mustang 2013

Ferrari 458 Italia AF Corse LM 2014

V8 Supercars

The full scale class is very popular in Australia and the RC version is typically any touring car shell painted in the livery of a V8 Supercar team:

2019 Holden Bathurst Special Livery (Jamie Whincup & Craig Lowndes)

2012 Holden Commodore VE

2008 Ford Falcon (Dick Johnson Racing)

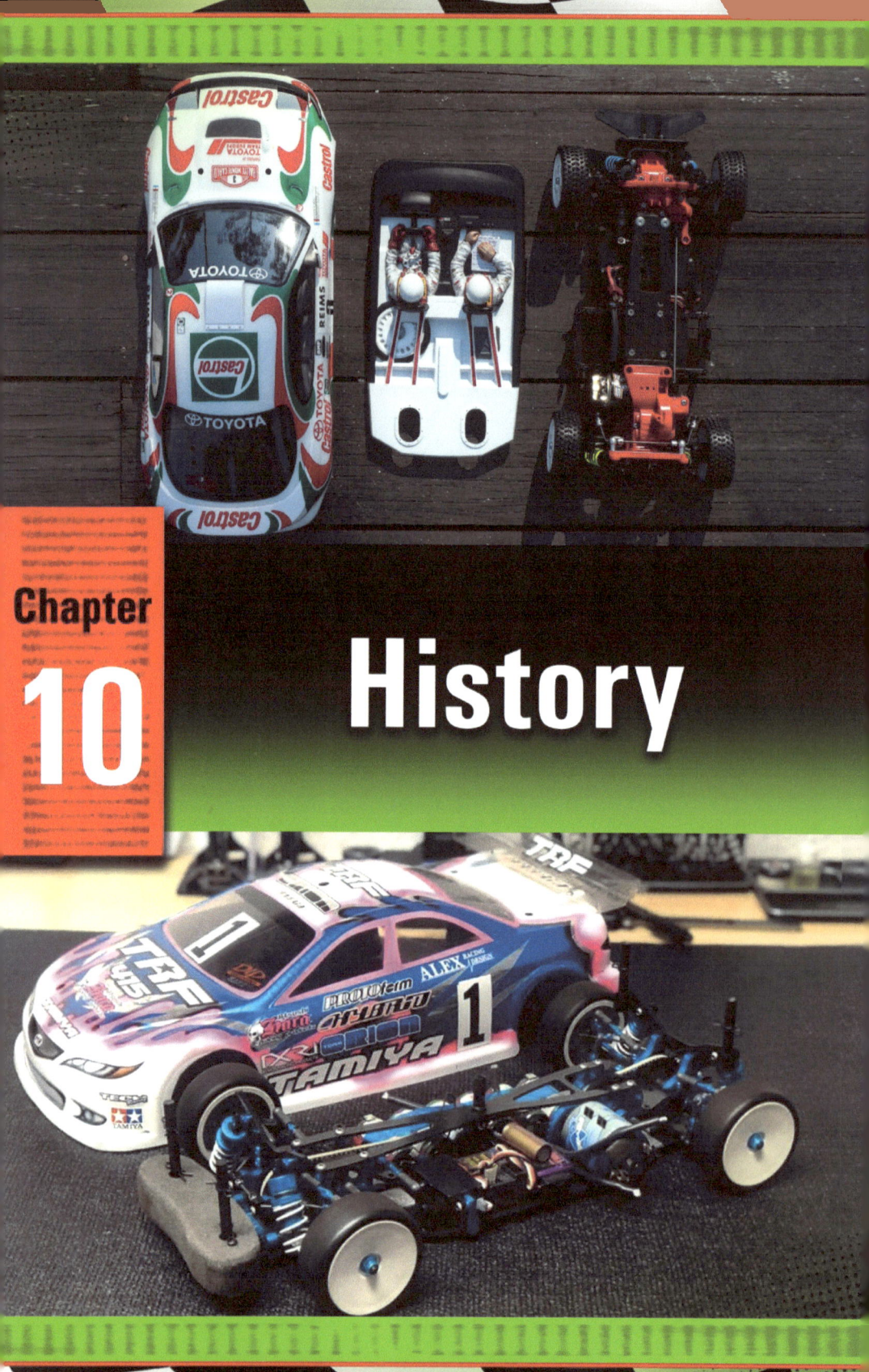

Chapter 10

History

*Craig Howard from **www.thercracer.com** takes us through the history of Touring Car development.*

The cars we race today are a product of decades of intense competition. I thought it would be interesting to cover the history of the class, and call out key milestones in its development by looking at each of the IFMAR ISTC World Championship winning chassis.

Background

1/10 on-road is a relative newcomer in the world of RC racing, before the nineties 1/12 scale pan cars were the only on-road option. You would expect these would act as the nucleus for the cars we race today, but actually its origins are rather different.

In the eighties, off-road buggy racing was really popular. The simple electric SRB's soon made way for more sophisticated race chassis. Then in 1995 Tamiya released the Hotshot creating a big impact with its affordable 4WD shaft driven design.

This new era of 4WD buggies also coincided with the golden era of Rally thanks to loads of TV coverage and the exotic Group B super cars. These two worlds collided to provide us with RC rally cross. These were 4WD buggies with wide 220mm rally car shells.

As winter approached, RC racing went indoors, so these Rally cross cars could be slammed lower. Many just modified the shocks on the 4WD buggies to adapt to the flat tracks, but there were some actual wide touring car kits released, such as the Schumacher Wildcat touring cars. These were very crude kits compared to the 4WD buggies, but they were cheap, so they helped make the class even more popular over the next few years. Although it was still a niche class compared to 1/10 off-road.

1991 Tamiya TA01 – the kit that started it all!

The big impact came in 1991 when Tamiya released 58096 Tamiya Toyota Celica GT-4. It introduced the TA01 chassis, derived from the Manta Ray DF-01 but with shorter suspension arms (190mm) and a lower stance. Tamiya released a slew of these cars in quick succession featuring a Skyline GT-R Nismo, Mercedes 190E Evo, and the BMW M3 sport.

The shells were a tremendous leap in quality compared to other manufacturers. The cars handled really well and importantly, they were cheap. Many racers flocked to this new class, as it also had the advantage that it could be raced indoors and out. The 1/10 on-road class that we now know was born!

The class literally exploded within a year. Many off-road racers bought a TA01 to race in the winter months, and when spring arrived decided that it was more fun racing these cars and abandoned buggy racing. I was one of those people. It was a great time, and my local club tripled in size as it was really simple to join in the fun. For anyone interested in joining the hobby you just told them that the Tamiya was the only option, so they simply had to choose the shell they liked the most and get started.

History **10**

1993 Tamiya TA02 — the first race spec Tamiya

Tamiya released the TA02 in 1993. It was very close to the TA01 and shared many of the same parts. The key differences were focused on improving the steering and weight balance. It had updated front arms and hubs, and the chassis was shorter, moving the battery forward.

The original came with an analog speed controller (not pictured)

Castrol Toyota Celica (1993 Monte-Carlo Rally Winner)
Aftermarket driver/navigator model pictured

1996 — The rise of the competition — HPI RS4

HPI was a small company that made a popular chassis conversion for the TA02, but they were not content with just making hop-ups. The designers were working on a car that some would call the first proper race spec chassis, the RS4.

The RS4 was a superb car with its belt drives signalling a big change to the shaft cars popular at that time. With kit bearings, universal drive shafts, adjustable shocks and geometry, all included in the box, people had to take notice.

The original RS4 with two speed transmission

The World Championships

By 1998, 1/10 on-road was so popular that there was a lot of demand for it to be included in the IFMAR worlds roster. Due to this demand it was decided that there would be a provisional race to go alongside the 1/12 and Pro 10 classes. All the manufacturers assembled their top drivers to put their new chassis through its paces in the first world championship touring race.

History 10

1998 Losi Street Weapon IWC — Driver: David Spashett

David Spashett won the inaugural world Touring Car championship with the Losi Street weapon. He also won the 1/12 and Pro 10 classes at the same event. The only time a driver has ever achieved such a feat!

David Spashett's history making cars. From left to right, 1/12th, Pro 10 and Touring Car

The Street Weapon was a great car, designed by the legendary Gil Losi. The car has a very distinctive layout as you can see in the picture below. With the motor upfront the car had a significant amount of on-power steering for the time. The chassis was adapted from the XX-4 buggy, but the revised suspension geometry really made the car shine on the track.

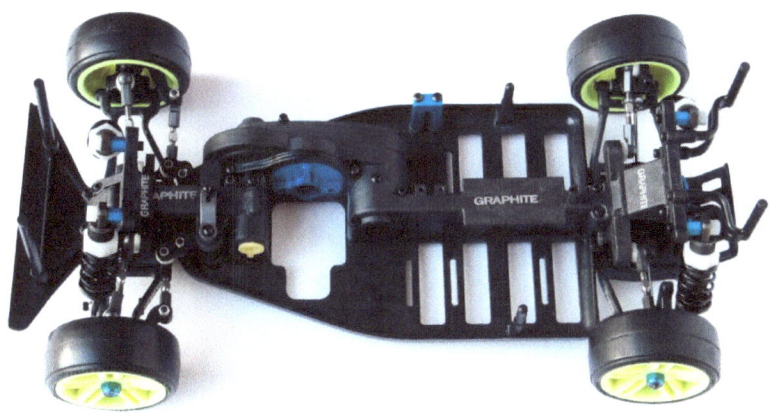

Soon there was a special IWC world's edition released with lots of optional goodies.

2000 Yokomo MR4 TC – Driver: Atsushi Hara

The Yokomo MR4 was released in late 1999. It was originally intended to be an entry level car released alongside the YR-4 which was Yokomo's 'Pro' chassis. The car was fantastic, and it had a good level of specification for the time, with full ball bearings, ball diffs with lightweight outdrives and an efficient belt driven drive train.

It was not only club racers who noticed the potential of the car, Yokomo team drivers at the time Barry Baker and Masami Hirosaka tried the chassis and found that the car was much more consistent to drive fast than the YR-4.

Yokomo took the team driver's feedback and soon released the MR4-TC Pro kit. This had a lot more hop-ups included, such as threaded shocks, turnbuckles, revised steering assembly and a new top deck to make the car stiffer.

The millennium race was hosted at the Yatabe Arena in Japan. This world championship was a much bigger affair as Touring cars had become the most popular class worldwide. The winner was Atsushi Hara, driving the Yokomo MR4 TC.

This led to the release of a world's edition kit which provided the following changes:

- Graphite chassis tub
- Worlds upper deck
- Worlds front & rear suspension arms
- Centre one way & front drive pulley
- Titanium turnbuckles
- Front roll bar
- Aluminium driveshafts

The MR4 went on to be a popular platform for Yokomo, and a shaft drive variant was released (the SD) which is still popular with some drifters. The Yokomo is the only tub chassis to have won the worlds, although later versions of the MR4 would move to a carbon double deck.

2002 Tamiya TRF414M — Driver: Surikarn Chaidejsuriya

In 2002 the event took place in South Africa, here Surikarn Chaidejsuriya surprised the crowds and took Tamiya's first world championship.

Despite being the pioneers of the 190mm touring car class with their affordable TA01 and TA02 cars, Tamiya soon fell behind as the class became more popular and specialist race cars were built by rival manufacturers.

In 1998, Tamiya decided they wanted to create a car that would put them back in contention and their design team of Masayuki Miura, Takanori Aoki and Takahiko Yasui started developing the TRF404X.

This prototype had a two belt design with the motor central at the rear of the car, and saddle packs placing the weight in the centre of the chassis. It was soon apparent that the chassis had real potential, and the design team were given the budget to create many prototypes and the final result was the TRF414.

There were a few revisions to the chassis, the bulkheads were changed to allow roll bars to be fitted, and the decks were revised with the batteries being moved for better steering response.

Surikarn drove the world's edition of the TRF414M which had lightened bulkheads making the car more responsive. It also had revised suspension mounts and a different front roll bar kit.

The TRF414 M2 was the first TRF kit that came in the distinctive TRF blue. There were many cars that had similar layouts to the TRF414 including the Xray T1.

2004 Tamiya TRF415MS — Driver: Marc Rheinard

The 2004 championship was held in Florida. World champion Surikarn was using the Tamiya TB Evolution IV and a young Marc Rheinard drove the latest TRF415MS chassis and claimed the winner's trophy.

Tamiya had come back as reigning champions and reclaimed their crown (the only manufacturer to do that until Yokomo in 2016). The TRF415 was a significant chassis as it sported a very different layout and design from the previous TRF414 and kits from the other manufacturers. It would prove to be the blueprint for most future touring cars.

The TRF415 was a collaboration between Tamiya Japan and Tech Racing. Tech Racing had been making some interesting conversions for other manufacturer's chassis, along with releasing their own club cars.

The Tech racing MY02 and the TRF415 share a lot of common design features, and the drive train was interchangeable. There was a large gap in build quality, however, and also the suspension arms on the 415 were different and had much better geometry.

History 10

The drive train was a dual belt system with a ball diff in the rear and a one-way in the front. This would be the standard for some time.

The original TRF415 had 3 top decks, one along the chassis and the other two for the front and rear stiffeners. This chassis was built in a time when flex was not a design consideration, and this car was stiff. It was also epic on foam tyres. Although, soon people would come to race without the side stiffeners.

As the car was developed, Tamiya fitted a range of new parts, including the reversible lightweight suspension and shock towers, lightened motor mount and a thinner bottom deck (2.5mm as opposed to the 3mm original).

This MS spec car took the championship, although there was a lot more evolution to come from the TRF415 platform.

2006 Hot Bodies Cyclone — Driver: Andy Moore

In 2006, the championship was held in Italy at the Collegno Track. Here HPI took the crown with their Hot Bodies Cyclone.

The Cyclone is probably one of the most under-rated cars, in my opinion. It was one of the first cars to move all the weight towards the middle of the car using the conventional layout that we have now. The belt pulleys were on either side of the spur gear. The aluminium rear mount kept the chassis flex under control with a low turn brushed motor, but also allowed the batteries to fit closer to the centre of the chassis. The car also had easy to adjust Ackermann on the steering arms.

The suspension was from the Pro4, and this car was the first proper Hot Bodies chassis. The big difference was the Cyclone was much easier to drive.

2008 Tamiya TRF416WE — Driver: Marc Rheinard

Now over to Bangkok for the 2008 worlds. In a memorable final showdown, Marc Rheinard pushed Hara to claim victory whilst driving the Tamiya TRF416 WE. The race is a classic, and it really showcases the reasons this class is so popular.

The winning car was an evolution of the TRF416 that was released a year earlier in 2007. The TRF416 inherited all the key features of the TRF415 chassis line and took it further to have better left and right balance by moving the motor in a considerable amount. It also was a lot lighter as the large rear aluminium bulkheads were disposed of and a separate motor mount was introduced, providing a little more flex and giving the car a lot of mechanical grip.

The World Edition version of the TRF416 had a longer top deck which gave the car more flex, as racing chassis moved away from the mantra of stiff is best. This gave a more neutral chassis. It had Tamiya's short reversible suspension arms, and with the battery moved forward these gave the car even better response on the track. It also featured a spool as standard (brushless motors killed the one-ways that were popular up to that time). The car was very popular at club level, as it was easy to drive and really quick out of the box.

2010 Tamiya TRF416X — Driver: Marc Rheinard

Burgdorf in Germany was the setting for the 2010 championship, and the Tamiya team took victory again thanks to Marc Rheinard. Giving Marc three championships and Tamiya an unprecedented four world titles.

The 416X had quite a few tweaks ensure that the 416 could cope with the advancements of lipo and brushless technology. The motor position was mounted further back for extra traction under acceleration. It was also more central for better overall chassis balance and corner transitioning.

*All of Marc Rheinard's winning cars,
From left to right: Tamiya 415MS (2004), 416WE (2008) and 416X (2010)*

2012 Tamiya TRF417v5 — Driver: Jilles Groskamp

At the MACH circuit at Heemsteed in the Netherlands, Jilles Groskamp took a popular win at this home circuit with the TRF417x.

The TRF417 itself had gone through a pretty quick rate of change from its initial launch only a year earlier. Flex was the main reasoning behind the changes, as it was the era when the concept of controlled, even, flex was becoming paramount to chassis design.

The original car had a solid rear-motor mount (soon to be cut by many asphalt racers to obtain more flex), the chassis had lots of cut-outs that were different on each side of the lower deck and the servo was mounted in the conventional way with two posts.

The TRF417x was a big jump to moving the flex around on the car. The motor mount was in two parts, and the chassis was softer and revised to have a floating servo mount. This gave the car much more flex (although not enough for some, who fitted conversions to have even more).

The other distinctive feature about the world's car is that it uses aeration shocks, these do not have a bladder like the standard shocks, and they let out air in the caps to allow you to build cars with negative rebound, ideal for the low traction surface / tyre combination that was used at this world final.

The released version of the car is called the V5 not the X, to celebrate 5 Victories for the Tamiya TRF team.

2014 Yokomo BD7 15 — Driver: Naoto Matsukura

Back to the Full throttle raceway in Florida, the host of the 2004 worlds. This time it was not about Tamiya but the two leading Yokomo drivers, Ronald Völker and Naoto Matsukura, as they battled for victory.

The car that was dominating was the BD7 2015 edition. The original BD7 prototype was raced at the 2012 worlds and was a big step forward from the previous car. Yokomo had invested heavily on the on-road scene and the BD7 took a lot of its design inspiration from rival cars, but importantly it also brought some big innovations of its own, including the motor mount which brought the motor much closer to the centre of the car.

The world's car had a few interesting changes, such as a motor mount that could be set into two positions (forward or backwards) depending on how much grip was available at the track. It is also worth noting this chassis featured an oil filled gear differential in the rear (replacing the ball differential). Gear differentials have no slip and provide a little more speed off the line.

Other changes were shorter suspension arms, and a battery tape system that helps keep the flex of the chassis even more symmetrical than standard taping methods.

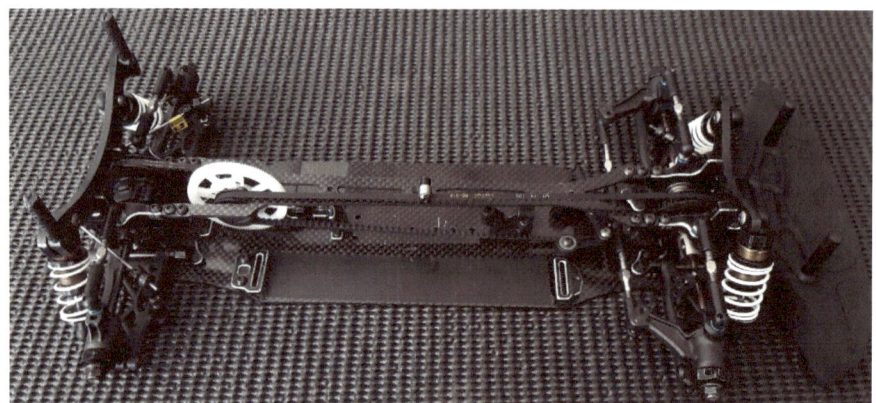

2016 Yokomo BD8 — Driver: Ronald Völker

Yokomo was on top of the world, and they kept the momentum by winning the 2016 event in China with the Yokomo BD8.

It was a departure from the BD7 with a lot of revisions. Smaller differentials to lower the centre of gravity and a refined drive train with a centre aligned front belt moving the motor a whopping 2mm inboard to improve car stability. The new suspension mount system also allowed for the driver to change the settings to suit conditions, something that the Yokomo team insisted really helped them as the track conditions evolved over the course of the world's event.

ARS (Active rear suspension) is another feature and one that was used to help Ronald have more grip and rear traction in Beijing. ARS works by adding a level of bump steer to the rear wheels; as the suspension compresses, the rear toe changes.

There are other new parts such as C-Hubs, uprights, and the lower plate has had the flex points changed.

2018 Xray T4'18 — Driver: Bruno Coelho

The 2018 worlds were held at the Welkom RC Arena in South Africa. This indoor facility was superb, unfortunately the location was not. Some of the large factory teams and support engineers did not attend due to safety concerns.

The event would still host some great racing amongst fierce competitors. Defending champion Ronald Völker top qualified with the runner up from the last two championships, Bruno Coelho, alongside him in P2.

As the finals commenced, the two drivers were very close with Ronald making his Yokomo very wide until Bruno managed a pass and claimed A1. In the second final the Yokomo did not have the grip and Bruno managed to pass Ronald on the third lap. He never looked back and claimed his, and Xray's, first world championship.

Xray, founded by Juraj Hudy, started manufacturing competitive racing chassis in late 2000 when they introduced the T1 to the world. They have become one of the most popular brands in the RC racing community.

The Xray T1 had a layout very similar to other popular chassis of the day and included pivotballs on the arms that would allow you to adjust the camber and caster easily. However, the added weight over the wheels could cause the caster to move during large impacts.

The 2018 world's winning chassis was based on the Xray T4'18 with some prototype parts that would later feature in the T4'19 chassis. This chassis reflects many of the current trends with chassis design. The dampers are now even shorter in their Ultra Low Profile guise (15mm shorter than those on the original T1).

Bruno's chassis also featured active rear suspension, which reduces the rear toe-in on the straights. Chassis flex was developed further with inline flex options seen on the earlier TRF and Yokomo cars. Interestingly, this is the first world's winner that ran an aluminium chassis. These have become more common because of the rise of very high grip carpet tracks around the globe, combining stiffness with the benefit of adding weight lower to the ground.

2020

Unfortunately, the 2020 World Championship was postponed due to the Covid-19 pandemic.

With the increase of high grip racing, we have seen motors move from rear mounts to closer to the middle of the chassis, in the never-ending pursuit of improved handling and higher corner speed. Interestingly, the Tamiya TA05 (2005) was a mid-motor chassis. Old ideas become new again. Modern electrics such as shorty lipos and 1/12 scale high power servos may lead to new chassis layouts for better weight balance.

In the world of RC racing, nothing stands still. All of our favourite brands are working hard to claim the top spot. What new trends will emerge? It will be interesting to see what the future holds.

Appendix A — eBook

This book is available as an eBook at a discount to those that have already purchased the physical book.

The eBook is available for any device with a web browser: Windows and Mac, iOS and Android, etc.

Additional eBook features include:

- Full-text search.
- Annotate content, including:
    - Highlight text.
    - Add your own notes to any text.
- Annotations are available across all of your devices, i.e., make notes on your phone and they are available on your tablet and computer.
- Cross-referencing is hyperlinked.

Visit www.DaveBStevens.com for details and to purchase.

Appendix B — Glossary

This section explains the common terms used in this book, where they are not otherwise explained as part of the relevant chapter.

For a diagram of car parts refer to page 89.

A-arm	Another term for suspension arm.
Aggressive	An aggressive car has a greater steering response initially.
Chunking	Foam tyres may lose a chunk of foam, often on the outside of the rim. This is called chunking. Causes include: a crash, car-to-car contact, or if a tyre is no longer correctly glued to the rim (as the edge of the tyre may lift during cornering).
Corner Entry	Corner entry is when you first turn-in to a corner until you stop turning the steering wheel on your radio. The car begins to roll, and this sets up the line to be taken through the corner. It is often defined as the segment of the turn from the turn-in point to the apex.
Corner Exit	Corner exit is where you are reducing the steering input and commence accelerating. The car starts to roll back level. It is often defined as the segment of the turn from the apex until the corner has been completed.
cSt	Centistokes (cSt) is a measurement of oil viscosity (typically shock oil and diff oil). It is a standard unit of measurement which can be compared between manufacturers. Another common measurement is Weight (Wt, WT or just W). However, Weight is not a standard unit of measure and therefore cannot be compared between manufacturers.

CVD	Used to refer to a driveshaft with Constant Velocity Drive (CVD). The constant velocity joint allows the driveshaft to transmit power to the wheels even when the wheels are turning into a corner. The greater the steering angle, the greater the forces on the CVD's joint, and this can cause wheel vibration, and resulting noise, as the wheel approaches full steering lock (called "Chatter".) A DCJ can be used instead of a CVD to reduce or eliminate "chatter" (refer to DCJ below.) On high-end racing kits, DCJs are used on the front while CVDs are used on the rear.
DCJ	Used to refer to a driveshaft with a Double Cardan Joint (DCJ). A DCJ has two joints in the driveshaft and is more effective at reducing or eliminating "chatter" than a CVD (refer to CVD above for an explanation of "chatter".) On high-end racing kits, DCJs are used on the front while CVDs are used on the rear.
DNF	Did Not Finish a race that the car started.
DNS	Did Not Start in a race that the car entered.
Dog Bones	Entry-level kits sometimes use driveshafts called dog bones. They are not as effective as CVDs and are not attached to the drivetrain, so might come out in a crash which damages the drivetrain.
ESC	The Electronic Speed Controller (ESC) controls the speed and direction of the motor.
Forward Traction	Forward traction is how much grip you have when accelerating in a forward direction.
ISTC	International Scale Touring Car (ISTC).
Loctite	Loctite is a brand of thread locker which has become a generic term for any brand of thread locking liquid. It is used on screws where they are screwed into aluminium. The Loctite cures into a plastic that locks the threads together, preventing the screw from working loose from vibration. The screw can still be unscrewed using a driver or screwdriver. Do not use Loctite when screwing into plastic as you may not be able to unscrew it again.

Glossary - Appendix B

Loose	Loose is another word for Oversteer.
Mid-corner	Mid-corner is the part of the corner where steering input is constant (the steering wheel is turned at a constant angle and is neither increasing nor decreasing). The car is at maximum roll. The apex is normally taken during the mid-corner (refer to page *25*).
Off-power Steering	This is when trying to change the direction of the car while the throttle is neutral or under braking. Letting off the power causes the car to dive at the front and rise at the rear. Braking causes this effect to increase, i.e., the car dives more at the front under braking.
On-power Steering	This is when trying to change the direction of the car while holding or increasing the throttle. For example, coming out of a slow corner and then accelerating through a sweeper, the driver is accelerating while changing the steering angle. Under power, the car will rise at the front and squat at the rear.
Oversteer (Loose)	Oversteer is a cornering situation where the rear wheels do not track behind the front wheels but instead slide out toward the outside of the turn. Oversteer can cause the car to spin. Put simply, when you turn into a corner, oversteer is when the car turns more than you expected. It is often referred to as the car being 'loose' or where the driver 'loses' the back-end. Rear wheel drive cars are generally more prone to oversteer than 4WD, in particular when applying power in a tight corner. This occurs because the rear tyres must handle both the lateral cornering force and engine torque. Sudden weight transfer, such as swerving, can cause oversteer. For solutions to oversteer refer to the checklist for *Too Much Steering (Oversteer)* on page *256*.
Push	Push is another word for Understeer.

236

Slip Angle	Slip angle is the angle between a rolling tyre's actual direction of travel and the direction which it is pointing. In other words, it's the difference between where the tyre is pointing and where it's actually going.
Turns (Motors)	The number of turns in a motor is the number of times the copper wire has been wound around the armature. The higher the number of turns the greater the torque but the lower the RPM. The lower the RPM the slower the top speed. For example, a 21.5 motor is normally slower than a 17.5 motor. Motors can also be rated by kV. A motor with a higher kV will have higher RPM but less torque.
Understeer (Push)	Understeer is a cornering situation where the car turns less sharply than the driver intends. This typically occurs when the front tyres have insufficient traction for the car to follow the intended line. Put simply, when you turn into a corner, understeer is when the car turns less than you expected. It is also often referred to as 'pushing', or refusing to turn-in. Too much speed when entering a corner can also cause understeer. It is common for a manufacturer's base setup to have a slight tendency to understeer by default. If a car understeers slightly, it tends to be more stable (for drivers of average ability). For solutions to understeer refer to the checklist for *Not Enough Steering (Understeer)* on page *258*.
Viscosity	Viscosity is the thickness of the oil. It is measured in cSt (a standard unit of measurement which can be compared between manufacturers) or Wt (which cannot be compared between manufacturers).
Wishbone	Another term for suspension arm.

Appendix C — Beginner's Guide

If you are a complete beginner, and have just bought your first car (or are about to), then the content of this book may seem overwhelming at first.

To assist, this appendix assumes you know nothing about RC cars or racing and provides knowledge which is assumed elsewhere in this book. It also highlights some common rookie mistakes to avoid.

Buying Considerations

Key considerations when buying a touring car include:

1. **Who else runs it at your local track?** — If another racer has a car that handles well, and is prepared to share their ideas, then buying the same model of chassis may be a smart move. So an early step is to visit your local track and talk to other racers.

2. **Parts availability** — If parts are on the shelf at your local hobby shop, then that's a big advantage when you break something. Next would be an online store with fast shipping. If you can't find a store that stocks parts, either locally or online, then don't buy the kit.

3. **Online Community** — Is there a strong online community where you can ask questions, share setups, and see what issues other drivers are experiencing? This may also be a great place to look for reviews.

4. **Second-Hand** — Buying second-hand means no manufacturer's warranty and parts might be bent or missing. The price needs to reflect this risk. However, buying from a respected local racer can be a great way to get a bargain. If they race at your club, they are more likely to sell you a reasonable car.

5. **Minimum Specification**

	Cheaper Cars	Recommended
Chassis & Shock Towers	Plastic or FRP	Carbon Fibre
Shock Absorbers	Foam filled, with spacer collars for adjustment	Oil filled with screw thread collars for adjustment
Screws	Various	Metric hex screws
Bearings/Bushings	Bushings	Ball Bearings

A Beginner's Story

I started RC car racing in 2007 in the Novice class at my local track. The class featured restricted gearing to keep speeds reasonable for beginners.

My first car was a Tamiya TL-01 (since discontinued). This was an entry level car and was designed for tearing up and down the local street rather than winning at the local track. To put it in perspective, the entire ready to run package cost me less than a mid-range ESC. It wasn't competitive, but it gave me the RC bug and taught me some basics. My son Aaron had a similar car. We both had so much fun!

There were typically a dozen entries in the Novice class each race day, and I didn't do very well initially. However, six months later I won the Novice Summer Season championship.

When I started, just trying to complete one circuit of the track without crashing many times seemed incredibly difficult. With perseverance, I gradually got better. I was no longer coming last, but I was nowhere near the race leaders. What to do? I did a lot of reading and decided to invest in a new ESC. This did seem to make the car a little quicker, but in hindsight wasn't the best use of my money. I tried a lot of things to make the car quicker and handle better, most of which were not time or money well spent. If I were starting again, these would be my top tips to myself, as a beginner:

1. If your car uses bushings instead of ball bearings, then changing these is your first priority. Bearings will enhance performance, reliability, and run time.

2. Buy two reasonable quality Lipo batteries. You should go noticeably faster compared to the NiMH batteries that come with most Ready to Run (RTR) kits. You can get away with one battery, but having two makes life much easier. It also ensures you should be able to start every race with a full battery. This is important because batteries lose voltage as they discharge and lower voltage means less speed. Note: you will need a charger capable of handling Lipo batteries. Charging a Lipo battery with a non-Lipo charger is extremely dangerous.

3. Tamiya RTR cars are still popular today, but they come with Tamiya plugs between the ESC and battery. These tend to come loose, fault or melt, and don't conduct electricity as well as other connectors. I use Deans Ultra Plugs or bullet connectors. There is nothing more frustrating than your car stopping in the middle of the race with a problem that could have been prevented. Changing plugs between the battery and ESC can save a great deal of frustration.

4. Make sure the on/off switch is easy to get at with the body on. However, don't mount it on the chassis with the switch protruding because the car might get turned off in a crash. Very frustrating!

5. If you have a belt-driven car, loosen the belt as much as possible. The motor shouldn't produce enough power to make the belt skip, but loosening it reduces friction and makes the car quicker. When loosening belts make sure they don't drag against the chassis or other components.

6. Buy a body designed for racing. They may not look as cool, but there is an advantage to how your car will handle. Refer to page 80.

7. Having difficulty turning the wheel on the radio the correct amount to get around corners? Turn down the dual rate setting on your radio. Some RTR radios don't have dual rate, in which case an upgrade is recommended. Even a mid-level radio makes driving much easier when compared to an RTR radio.

8. Practice! To finish first, first you must finish. In the beginner class it's not necessarily the fastest car that wins but the car that gets around the track with the least number of crashes!

At that stage I knew I loved RC racing, but wasn't ready to spend a lot of money. So I bought a second-hand car from a local, one that was designed to race (whereas my old car was more of a basher). He was buying the latest model and wanted to sell his current car. I simply transferred the electronics from my old car. This worked out very well, and I found the new car to be significantly easier to drive. Money well spent!

A car designed to race, plenty of practice, and the other tips I've noted in this appendix allowed me to become competitive.

Practice — talk to people at the club and ask their advice — and have fun!

Common Build Errors

1. Reversed C-hubs

The C-Hubs set the Caster on the car. C-Hubs always lean towards the back of the car. If you put the left C-Hub on the right-hand side of the car, then it will lean towards the front of the car. This will cause unpredictable handling. With on-road cars it is an easy mistake to make, as the angle is typically only a few degrees and can be difficult to see. The C-Hub below is on the left hand suspension arm and leans to the rear of the car (towards the right of the photo):

2. Shocks are not the same left-to-right

The length of the shock absorbers from tip to tip must be the same on the front left as on the front right. Similarly, the length of the rear left must be the same as the rear right. Differences in length will cause unusual handling. Refer to page *106* for more information.

3. Setting ride height incorrectly

Some new drivers use the droop screws to set the ride height by mistake (I know I did). This will cause handling problems. Droop screws are used to adjust droop, not ride height.

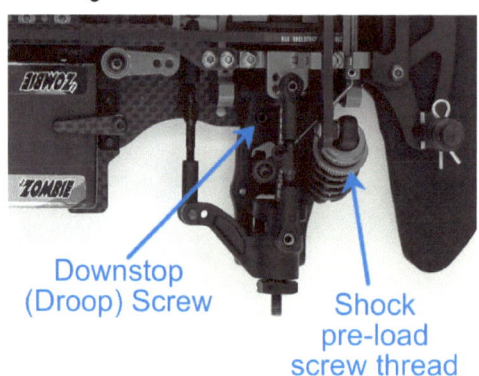

Downstop (Droop) Screw   Shock pre-load screw thread

Ride height is set by compressing the shock springs. This might be achieved via a screw thread at the top of each shock, or your car might use plastic spacers installed between the spring and the top of the shock.

- The setting of the **front** left shock must be the same as the **front** right shock.

- The setting of the **rear** left shock must be the same as the **rear** right shock.

- Front shocks and rear shocks may have different settings.

For example, if you screw down 1mm on the left front shock (or install a 1mm spacer on the left front shock) then do the same on the right front shock. Failure to adjust shocks the same left-to-right can cause unpredictable handling.

Don't try to make the ride height the same on both sides of the chassis. Ride height is typically measured at the centreline of the chassis (i.e., at the middle of the front of the chassis and at the middle of the rear of the chassis). If you have a car which is perfectly balanced left-to-right (refer to page *157*) then the left side and the right side of the chassis should be a similar height. However, this won't always be the case and is nothing to be concerned about at this early stage (once you gain more experience you can correct this issue by referring to the chapter on *Tweak*).

Refer to page *134* for detailed instructions on setting the ride height. Refer to page *119* for an explanation of the droop screws.

4. Unequal Droop

Droop is measured using a droop gauge and droop blocks. However, the most important thing for beginners to ensure is that the droop is the same left-to-right on both the front and rear of the car. Otherwise unpredictable handling can result.

If you have a droop gauge (or a ruler) then set your droop using the instructions on page *119*.

If you do not have a droop gauge (and have difficulty with the ruler method) then unscrew all four droop screws (one per suspension arm) so they are not touching the chassis. This amount of droop is greater than optimal, however, it will be equal side-to-side, which is more important. The photo on the previous page shows the droop screw (also called downstop screw) location. I recommend buying a droop gauge and you can see examples on page *119*.

A quick visual check of droop is to place the race ready car (body off) on a flat surface and push down on the top of the shock in one corner of the car until the chassis touches the surface. The tyre on the diagonally opposite corner should remain in contact with the surface. If it doesn't, then the tyre that lifted off the surface needs more droop. Repeat the test for all four corners of the car.

5. **Gear mesh too tight or too loose**

The pinion gear is the gear attached to the motor. The gap between the pinion gear and the spur gear is the gear mesh. If the gear mesh is too tight, then your car will not be fast and you will burn out motors more easily. The slower the motor, the larger the gear mesh gap is able to be without causing problems. However, if the gear mesh is too loose, the plastic spur gear could strip and leave your car stranded. Refer to page *128* for more information.

Too loose
(In this photo the pinion gear is on the right, but this doesn't matter. What's important is the gap between the pinion gears teeth and the spur gears teeth).

Just right
(Pinion gear is on the left).

6. **Level surface**

Use a reasonably level surface when checking ride height, camber and droop. If the surface is not level, then it may skew the settings (depending how far out of level it is). Note: flat and level are two different things. You are looking for both. A kitchen bench is usually flat and level. A pit table might be flat but may not be level (of course it may not be flat either, and that's why you'll see most racers using a setup board or piece of glass).

7. **Belt tensioning / tightness**

A belt that is too tight will cause strain on the drivetrain and motor. A belt that is too loose may rub against the chassis. When starting out belts should be as loose as practical without rubbing against the chassis. Some entry-level cars are shaft driven and some do not allow changing the belt tension. Check your car's manual. Refer to page 96 for more information.

8. Securing the battery

At most on-road races you will see a battery come out of a touring car reasonably regularly. Most of these situations are preventable. Make sure your battery is tightly secured. Ask the people at your club who don't lose batteries for some tips.

9. Completely free steering

When you disconnect the steering servo from the front wheels, the wheels should turn completely freely (and I mean you can move the wheel backwards and forwards with the slightest pressure from your little finger). If you can't, then something is binding. Ask someone at your club for advice on how to fix this.

10. Car keeps rolling over (traction rolling)

Ride height is probably too high. Refer to page 134 for recommended ride height. If your ride height is correct, then refer to the Traction Rolling Checklist on page 260.

11. Blowing motors

A common way of going faster is to turn the motor end bell timing up as far as it will go and drop the gearing to maximise speed on the straight, right? This is a great way to blow your motor. Refer to page 126 for detailed instructions on maximising your speed without burning out motors.

12. Battery not charged

Most beginner's start with one battery and quickly buy a second one. A common error is to forget to charge the battery you are using for the next race. To prevent this from happening, develop a system that works for you.

You might:

    a. Check the voltage of your battery before each race.

    b. Always store uncharged batteries in a lipo bag marked "Not charged" or conversely, store charged batteries in a lipo bag marked "Charged".

c. Designate a place on your pit table for uncharged batteries and when you remove the battery from the car, put it in this area.

13. Wiring the ESC backwards or plugging the battery wires in backwards — boom!

Unlike most battery chargers, your ESC does not contain protection circuitry from connecting the + cable to the – terminal (or vice versa). Running power through your ESC the wrong way, even for a millisecond, is the top reason that racers buy a new ESC (and the most frustrating).

So when soldering wires on your ESC, check twice and solder once.

If you use bullet connectors, then make sure the negative lead from the ESC is just long enough to reach the negative terminal of the battery, and that the positive lead from the ESC only just reaches the positive terminal of the battery. That way you can't connect them backwards (at least when the battery is installed in the car).

When buying a new battery that uses bullet connectors, double-check that the new battery has the + and – terminals on the same sides as your old battery. Not all manufacturers use the same layout!

14. Car veers to one side under power

There are two main possibilities:

a. The car has not been built the same way on the left side as on the right. This could be different shock lengths, different shock preload or the droop could be different. The setup for the front of the car should be the same left-to-right, and the setup for the rear of the car should be the same left-to-right. Refer to relevant sections of the chapters on The Build page 44 and Initial Setup page 69.

b. The car may be "tweaked". When I started out, I tended to crash a lot. Every crash has the potential to bend or break parts or to move components slightly out of alignment. If you can't see anything obvious, ask someone at your club for assistance, or refer to page *163* for instructions on how to diagnose this.

Tyre Gluing

Checking that your tyres have not come unglued should be part of your routine after every run. If a tyre needs regluing, there are many different techniques you might use. I recommend using very thin (runny) glue with an applicator that has a small hole and only allows a small amount of glue to flow.

Lay the tyre on a flat surface and run the glue around the circumference of the rim where it meets the tyre. The glue will find its way in between the rubber tyre and the wheel rim. With this technique you shouldn't get glue on your fingers, glue your finger to the tyre, or glue the tyre in the wrong position on the rim. So this is a good option, particularly for beginners. Make sure you choose thin CA glue and don't use so much that it pools on the side of the tyre.

If you use too much, quickly wipe away any excess with a rag, taking care that the excess doesn't run over the surface of the tyre.

Setup Diary

Take a notebook with you to the track and write down:

- your starting setup (most manufacturers provide a blank setup sheet for you to note this information. Fill it out and tape it into your notebook);
- each change made. Make one change at a time;
- any affect the change had. If you can't tell any difference, then undo the change before you try something else, and
- the track conditions at the time you made the change (track temperature, for asphalt is the track race ready or is it dirty).

This will help you understand what each adjustment does to your car's handling and will become a good reference tool for you.

I still have my setup diary for every car I've ever run.

Tools

You can save yourself a great deal of frustration trying to remove stripped screws by preventing them from stripping in the first place. This is achieved using a set of quality drivers where the tip is machined to fit the screw head precisely and is made of a hard metal which will not wear out quickly, such as this MR33 hex driver:

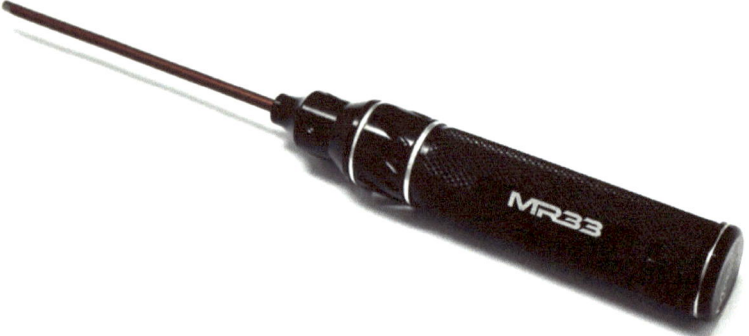

There are typically three types of screw heads used across the various manufacturers:

1. The most popular are hex heads using metric measurements, typically 1.5mm, 2mm, 2.5mm and 3mm.
2. Hex heads using imperial measurements, typically .050 inch, 1/16 inch, 5/64 inch and 3/32 inch.
3. Phillips or cross-head screws. These are predominantly used by Tamiya, a Japanese company, and Tamiya screws use the Japanese Industry Standard (JIS) screw head. Using a non-JIS screwdriver such as a Phillips screwdriver will often result in stripped screws.

Assuming your car uses metric drivers, then you will use the 2mm most frequently, followed closely by the 1.5mm. If you have a limited budget, you won't be sorry you spent the money on these drivers. The heads of the tools are usually replaceable and should be replaced whenever wear becomes noticeable.

Pinion gears are attached to the motor using a 1.5mm grub screw and tightening these sufficiently to not come off, while not stripping, can be a challenge with a cheap driver. If you do strip a pinion grub screw, take it to someone in the pits with a good quality hex driver, they may be able to get it out for you.

Lipo Battery Safety

Make sure you charge your lipo battery using a lipo charger, place the battery in a lipo safety bag during charging, and follow the manufacturer's advice on charge settings. Failure to follow basic safety guidelines can cause the battery to catch fire.

MR33 Lipo Safety Bag

Appendix D – Checklists

Quick Reference

Maintenance _____ 250
   After Run Checks _____ 250
   Between Events _____ 251
   Re-building a Car _____ 252
Correcting Key Balance Issues _____ 254
   Traction – How to Increase _____ 254
   Steering _____ 256
      Too Much Steering (Oversteer) _____ 256
      Not Enough Steering (Understeer) _____ 258
      Steering Response Changes for No Apparent Reason ___ 259
   Traction Rolling _____ 260
   Easier to Drive – How To _____ 261
Troubleshooting _____ 262
   Car Wanders on the Straight _____ 262
   Change of Direction (Chicane) _____ 262
   Fast Sweeper Cornering _____ 262
   Car 'Hops' or 'Chatters' Across the Track _____ 262
   Tyres Picking Up Carpet Debris from Track _____ 262
   Inconsistent Handling _____ 263
   Lacking Acceleration or Started Oversteering _____ 263

Checklists - Appendix **D**

Maintenance

After Run Checks

After a race or practice run, check your car over. The car should have a battery installed:

1. Check tyres:

   a. Are they still glued to their rims? Try and peel the tyre edge gently back with your thumb and if it comes away from the rim, add some CA glue to fix it in place. This applies for foam and rubber tyres. Foam tyres coming unglued can cause chunking.

   b. Look for cracks on the rim. If cracked, then replace, or CA glue may help for a short period.

   c. If foam tyres:

      i. Check for chunking (chunks of foam missing from the tyre).

      ii. Check for Tyre Coning, i.e., either the inside or outside of the tyre is wearing at a faster rate, causing the tyre to "cone". Check Camber and adjust as necessary to prevent coning (refer page 98).

      iii. Ride Height — The car's ride height decreases as foam tyres wear down to smaller diameters. Tyres may wear at different rates front-to-back and left-to-right, because the track may have more corners, or corners harder on the tyres, in one direction. This may cause a car with uneven ride height at all four corners. If necessary, swap tyres left-to-right to maintain even wear. Some racers will true tyres to maintain even ride height. Refer to Ride Height on page 134.

2. Check the wheel nuts are tight.

3. If your kingpins are screwed in from the bottom, check they haven't come loose.

4. Check the drive train is free by turning the spur gear with your finger — looking for any binding, belts rubbing on items that moved in the last race, gear mesh remains correct. Note: with high torque motors (stiff to turn), remove the pinion gear to check the drive train is free.

5. Check each of the wheels rotates as you'd expect — looking for drive wheels free wheeling or not turning freely.
6. Check each of the shocks pumps up and down as you'd expect — looking for leaks, ball joints popped off, springs not sitting correctly.
7. Check that all the electronic components are still secure — ESC, receiver, transponder, servo and haven't moved after a crash.
8. Push the front wheels to full lock in both directions and check for binding when the wheels turn.
9. Turn the car over and use a straight edge such as a steel ruler to check the chassis appears flat. If there is an issue refer to Tweak on page *163*.
10. Check the gear diff is not leaking/tightness of the ball diff (refer to page *115*).
11. If you had to change the steering trim during/after the race then the servo may have moved. Check the servo location and geometry (refer to pages *60* and *73*).

Some racers will put their car on a setup station after each run and partially disassemble the car to ensure it is operating correctly. This may identify further issues and, while not necessary after every run, it can be a good idea prior to a critical race.

Between Events

Even though your car is built perfectly (assuming you followed the advice in chapter 3), it won't stay perfect due to general wear and tear and unfortunate on track events. This happens to the best of us. This is why maintenance between race meetings is crucial to ensure the car stays in top-notch condition. Here's a simple checklist that I go through between race meetings to ensure my car maintains the best condition possible:

Element	What to Check
Chassis	Check there's no chassis tweak (on a flat surface), if there is then loosen top deck or bulkheads until tweak is removed, and re-tighten on a flat surface. Refer to page *164*.
Shocks	Shocks must contain no air and be consistent in rebound between all four. If not, then you must rebuild them and install new O-rings (I do this every time I rebuild shocks to ensure they are in the best possible condition). Follow the shock build guide on page *56* to restore your shocks back to perfect condition.

Suspension	Take your shocks off and ensure all suspension components are perfectly free and that none of the arms or hubs are binding. Also, check the roll bars to ensure they are still in tweak (page 58). Check for movement in suspension blocks and adjust if there is excessive slop.
Drivetrain	Remove DCJs and CVDs and clean with motor spray/degreaser. Re-lube with Muchmore V-Made Joint Lube/MR33 Joint Lube. Ensure no binding bearings, if binding then replace. Replace the rear driveshaft blades if worn. Check belts and pulleys for dirt and wear. Also check the spur gear for any wear and replace if necessary.
Setup	Double-check the setup to make sure it is applied properly. Check the camber, droop, ride height and EPA's to make sure the steering lock is still correct. Check your tweak and that your up-travel is still equal left and right. Refer to Initial Setup on page 70.

— Ryan Maker

Re-building a Car

If you buy a car second-hand, then we recommend stripping it down and building it as described in Chapters 3–5. Alternatively, here is a shorter, but less effective, checklist which beginners may find helpful:

1. Check the car to ensure it is not tweaked. Follow the instructions on page *163*.
2. Re-build the shocks (refer to page *56*).
3. Check that the front springs are both the same length and of the same type. Repeat for the rear springs.
4. Check the various shims which control the setup and ensure the same number and thickness of shims are used on both sides of the car (left = right).
5. Check the bearings spin freely.
6. Re-build the differential (refer to pages *53* and *115*).
7. Check the gearing (refer to page *126*).
8. Place the electronics but don't fix in place yet. Balance the car side-to-side and fix the electronics in place (refer to page *157*).

Essential Touring Car RC Racer's Guide

9. Check that the motor wires don't bind on the chassis or the body.
10. Program the ESC (refer to page *124*).
11. Program the radio (refer to page *132*).
12. Set the ride height (refer to page *134*).
13. Set the droop (refer to page *118*).
14. Re-check the ride height as changing the rear droop will change the ride height. If you change the ride height, re-check the rear droop.
15. Set the toe (refer to page *145*).
16. Set the camber (refer to page *98*).
17. Re-check the ride height as changing the camber will change the front ride height. If you change the ride height, re-check the camber.
18. When you first test the car, keep an eye on motor temperature (refer to page *129*).

Note that the above does not list every single setting that can be checked, but it is the minimum that we recommend.

Alexander Hagberg's car on the scrutineer's table at GP3F, Longwy, France

253

Correcting Key Balance Issues

Sometimes our cars have an inherent balance problem due to the style of the track or the amount of traction. Tracks can be so different that we need to make changes in order to make the car more gripped up, or in some cases take grip away, to make the car driveable. Here are the extreme situations where you may have a balance issue, and what to look for in order to get your car dialled!

— Ryan Maker

If you make a change and it does not improve the cars handling, then undo it before making the next change.

Traction — How to Increase

Having no traction on low grip tracks isn't much fun. There are ways of making the car work harder to generate traction from the tyres. Here are things you can do in order to make the car more aggressive and increase overall traction in low grip.

— Ryan Maker

Front and Rear Traction

Listed in the recommended order. Make one change at a time and check the result:

1. **Additive** — let it soak into tyres for longer and/or consider a second application. Page 153.
2. **Camber** — increase. Page 98.
3. **Ride height** — higher (within reason). Page 134.
4. **Shock position** — stand shocks up on shock tower (especially at rear). Page 109.
5. **Shock springs** — softer (rear first, then front if needed). Page 113.
6. **Shock oil** — softer. Page 107.
7. **Roll bar** — thicker front roll bar and/or thinner rear roll bar. Page 141.
8. **Flex** — increase (remove manufacturer recommended flex option screws). Page 125.
9. **Flex** — if available, add motor mount top deck flex post (can lock rear end in and prevent over-rotation, also more stable under braking).
10. **Diff height** — lower front and rear. Page 118.
11. **Roll centre** — lower front and rear. Page 142.

254

12. **Camber gain** — increase front and rear. Page *101*.

13. **Active rear toe** — if using, remove shim on outside hub for more link angle (more toe gain). Page *147*.

Rear Traction Only

1. **Diff (rear)** — gear diff thinner oil. Page *115*.

2. **Toe-in (rear)** — increase (2.5–3 degrees minimum). Page *147*.

3. **Ride height split** — decrease between front and rear. Page *134*.

4. **Wing** — to assist with higher speed corners, move the wing rearwards or use a high downforce wing (if local rules allow it). Page *87*.

5. For more rear traction ideas refer to *Oversteer* below.

Unexplained Loss of Traction

If your car has been handling well and then suddenly loses grip, here is a checklist of potential causes:

1. **Tyre temperature** (rubber tyres on asphalt) — are the tyres cold? — Make sure you do a couple of warm-up laps or use tyre warmers if necessary (page *155*).

2. **Track Temperature** — has the track temperature changed? Are the tyres you are using the correct ones for the new temperature?

3. **All tyres** — tyre gluing — check your tyres to see if any of them have come unglued.

4. **Differential** — is the gear diff leaking/ball diff still set correctly? Page *115*.

5. **Rear wing** — has the rear wing been damaged?

6. **Screws** — are all the chassis screws done up properly? Losing screws can cause unpredictable handling.

7. **Shocks** — are any of the shocks leaking?

8. **Droop** — is the droop still set correctly? Page *119*.

9. **Tweak** — has your car become tweaked? Page *163*.

Steering

Too Much Steering (Oversteer)

If the car has too much steering, it can be difficult to drive and may oversteer.

> Oversteer is an imbalance in the car with weight transfer biased towards the front. This means that the front is generating more traction than the rear. The aim when trying to achieve more rear traction is to add grip to the rear, not take too much traction away from the front. Rear traction is really important for forward drive, predictability and consistency. Not enough rear traction will cause you to be fighting your car throughout your runs. Here are some things you can do in order to achieve more rear traction in all grip levels.
>
> — Ryan Maker

Listed in the recommended order. Make one change at a time and check the result:

1. **Additive** — reduce on front tyres. Page *153*.
2. **Roll bar** — thicker front roll bar and/or thinner rear roll bar. Page *141*.
3. **Shock springs** — softer on rear first, then harder on front if needed. Page *113*.
4. **Shock oil** — thinner at rear first, then thicker on front if needed. Page *107*.
5. **Diff (rear)** — thinner gear diff oil in low grip or thicker oil in high grip. Page *115*.
6. **Ride Height** — as low as practical. Make the front ride height the same as the rear ride height. Page *134*.
7. **Droop** — more front droop and/or less rear droop. Page *119*.
8. **Camber** — decrease front first, then if needed increase rear. Page *98*.
9. **Toe-out (front)** — increase. Page *146*.
10. **Toe-in (rear)** — increase. Page *147*.
11. **Flex** — if available, add motor mount top deck flex post (can lock rear end in and prevent over-rotation, also more stable under braking).
12. **Shock Position** — stand rear shocks up on tower. Page *109*.
13. **Roll Centre** — lower the rear first, then raise the front. Page *141*.
14. **Track Width** — narrower rear (184–183mm). Page *149*.

15. **Radio** — reduce steering lock (dual rate). However, if the amount of steering is correct, but you'd like to reduce how quickly the car turns into the corner, then reduce the Steering Curve (Expo). Page *132*.

16. **Body Shell position** — move body shell backwards (more towards neutral). Page *82*.

17. **Bump Steer** — less shims. Page *97*.

18. **Camber Gain** — decrease. Page *101*.

19. **Wheelbase** — longer front and/or rear wheelbase. Page *161*.

20. **Weight** — if practical, move weight from the rear to the front (in front of battery and servo). Page *157*.

21. **Active Rear Toe** — if using, remove shim on outside hub for more link angle (more toe gain). Page *147*.

If the above do not resolve the oversteer then undo the changes, identify when the oversteer occurs and address as follows:

Oversteer at Corner Entry

1. **Track Width (front)** — wider. Page *149*.
2. **Track Width (rear)** — wider. Page *149*.
3. **Ackermann** — decrease. Page *89*.

Oversteer at Mid-corner

1. **Track Width (rear)** — wider. Page *149*.
2. **Wheel Base** — longer. Page *161*.

Oversteer at Corner Exit

Track Width (rear) — narrower. Narrower rear track width increases rear grip at corner exit. Page *149*.

Oversteer On-power

Spring (front) — softer spring to reduce on-power steering. Page *112*.

Not Enough Steering (Understeer)

Understeer is an imbalance in the car with weight transfer biased towards the rear. This means that the rear is generating more traction than the front. The aim when trying to achieve more steering is to add steering to the front, not take away traction from the rear. Rear traction is really important, for forward drive, predictability and consistency. However, a loose car (oversteering) is often a fast car, and having too much rear stability can slow you down and cause the car to bind up in the corners. Here are some things you can do in order to achieve more steering in all grip levels.

— Ryan Maker

Listed in the recommended order. Make one change at a time and check the result. If the car has insufficient steering:

1. **Ride height** — check the front ride height is lower than the rear ride height. Page 134.
2. **Additive** — increase on front tyres. Page 153.
3. **Roll bar (front)** — thicker, which makes the car feel more aggressive. Page 143.
4. **Shock springs** — softer on front first, then harder on rear if needed. Page 113.
5. **Shock oil** — thinner at front first, then thicker on rear if needed. Page 107.
6. **Shock position (rear)** — move bottom of shock towards the chassis on the suspension arm. Works better on smaller tracks. Page 109.
7. **Droop** — less front droop and/or more rear droop. Page 119.
8. **Camber** — increase. Page 98.
9. **Ride height split** — increase (within reason). Page 134.
10. **Diff (rear)** — gear diff thicker oil. Page 115.
11. **Front toe-out** — reduce. Page 146.
12. **Rear toe-in** — reduce. Page 147.
13. **Steering lock** — increase (but no more than 30 degrees for the inside wheel). Page 144.
14. **Track width (front)** — narrower (186–185mm). Page 149.
15. **Ackermann** — increase. Page 91.
16. **Bump steer** — more shims. Page 97.

17. **Flex** — increase (track dependant). Page 125.
18. **Camber gain (front)** — increase. Page 101.
19. **Wheelbase** — shorter. Page 161.
20. **Body shell position** — move further forward. Page 82.
21. **Wing position** — move wing further forward. Page 87.
22. **Weight** — remove weight from the front and/or add to the rear (behind battery and motor). Page 157.
23. **Active rear toe** — if using, add shim on outside hub for less link angle (less toe gain). Page 147.
24. **Roll centre (rear)** — if understeering on-power then raise the rear roll centre. Page 142.

Steering Response Changes for No Apparent Reason

If the car was steering correctly and no longer is, then:

1. Are the front linkages bent?
2. Are there any cracks, or loose screws, on any of the steering arms or parts?
3. Do the front arms move up and down on the springs and return to rest correctly?
4. If you disconnect the shocks are the suspension arms move completely freely?
5. Has the servo horn stripped?
6. Is the servo working correctly?
7. Is the car tweaked? (Refer to page 163).

Traction Rolling

Traction rolling is when the car is cornering, and it rolls over. It often occurs because the chassis has reached the limit of the amount it can roll, but needs to roll more. Because the chassis cannot roll any further, the car rolls over.

> Traction rolling can be just as annoying as having no traction. You do nothing wrong, but your car ends up in a wall at 80km/h ... great! It can be frustrating, but if you work through ways to decrease the risk of this, you can make your car less edgy, more enjoyable to drive and more consistent. Most traction rolling comes from the rear of the car.
>
> — Ryan Maker

Listed in the recommended order. Make one change at a time and check the result. To reduce or eliminate traction rolling:

1. **Ride height** — reduce. Page 134.
2. **Additive** — reduce traction additive on front tyres. Page 153.
3. **Additive** — shorten traction additive preparation time to 5 minutes or less. Page 153.
4. **Roll centre** — lower. Page 141.
5. **Roll bar (front)** — thinner (from 1.2 to 1.3mm). Page 140.
6. **Shock springs** — softer. Page 113.
7. **Shock oil** — thicker (as slows down weight transfer) start at rear. Page 107.
8. **Shock position** — lay the shocks over more on the shock tower. Page 109.
9. **Toe-out (front)** — increase (from 1.5 to 2 degrees each side). Page 146.
10. **Diff height** — raise front and rear. Page 118.
11. **Ride height split** — reduce (0.2–0mm). Page 134.
12. **Droop** — decrease rear droop and/or increase front droop. Page 119.
13. **Camber (front)** — reduce. Page 98.
14. **Camber gain** — decrease front and rear. Page 101.
15. **Weight** — move weight to the front of the car. If you have added weight at the back, move it in front of servo and battery. Page 160.
16. **Bump steer** — reduce shims. Page 97.
17. **Arm sweep** — add (up to 1 degree). Page 95.
18. **Glue front tyre sidewalls** — even a thin layer of glue helps stop the traction roll. This stiffens the sidewall and in some cases allows the tyre to

slide on the glue rather than fold under the car. Gluing the front sidewalls will reduce steering and may be best used on high grip carpet.

19. **Radio** — increase radio exponential and/or decrease steering lock (EPA or dual rate). Page *133*.
20. **Flex** — reduce, especially the front of the car (use top deck steering post). Page *125*.
21. **Ackermann** — reduce. Page *91*.

Easier to Drive — How To

Mid-mount cars are generally easier to drive than cars that have the motor rear mounted (refer to page *132*).

Listed in the recommended order. Make one change at a time and check the result:

1. **Toe-out (front)** — increase. Page *146*.
2. **Diff height** — high. Page *118*.
3. **Droop (rear)** — decrease. Page *122*.
4. **Roll bar (front)** — thinner. Page *140*.
5. **Camber** — decrease. Page *98*.
6. **Camber gain** — decrease. Page *101*.
7. **Ackermann** — reduce. Page *89*.
8. **Steering linkage angle** — increase. Page *144*.
9. **Caster** — increase. Page *104*.
10. **Weight balance (front-to-rear)** — move weight forwards if practical. Page *160*.
11. **Track width (rear)** — wider. Page *149*.
12. **Track width (front)** — wider. Page *149*.
13. **Wheelbase** — longer. Page *161*.
14. **Roll centre (rear)** — higher. Page *142*.
15. **Shock oil** — thicker. Page *107*.
16. **Shock rebound** — less rebound will make the car easier to drive on a bumpy track. Page *111*.
17. **Shock position on arm (rear)** — outside. Page *110*.

18. **Shock length** — increase. Page *106*.

Troubleshooting

Car Wanders on the Straight

1. **Toe-out (front)** — increase (page 146).
2. **Caster** — increase. Page *104*.

Change of Direction (Chicane)

If the car does not change directions quickly:

1. **Ride height** — lower, if practical. Page *134*.
2. **Ackermann** — reduce. Page *90*.
3. **Shock oil** — thicker. Page *107*.
4. **Diff height (rear)** — lower. Page *118*.
5. **Roll bar (rear)** — thicker. Page *140*.

Fast Sweeper Cornering

To increase steering through fast sweepers:

1. **Caster** — increase. Page *104*.
2. **Front toe-out** — reduce. Page *146*.
3. **Wheelbase** — increase. Page *161*.

Car 'Hops' or 'Chatters' Across the Track

If the car 'hops' (also called 'chatter' or 'judder') when cornering, then the springs are too stiff (refer to Springs on page *113*).

Tyres Picking Up Carpet Debris from Track

This is normally only an issue on the front tyres where the part of the tyre with traction additive is fine, but the unsauced tyre is picking up significant carpet debris, reducing steering partway through the race. To resolve, add traction additive to the rest of the front tyre and then reduce steering either by:

1. Refer to Too Much Steering checklist on page 256, or
2. Add CA glue to the sidewall of the front tyres which will take away steering.

Inconsistent Handling

The following issues can also cause inconsistent handling:

1. If the roll bars are not set correctly (refer to page 71).
2. Battery wires, ESC motor wires, motor sensor wire, should not interfere with the movement of the chassis or body.
3. Suspension arms should move up and down smoothly when the suspension is compressed.
4. Track width shims are the same on the left as on the right (refer to page 149).
5. Remove the front springs and place them next to each other on a flat surface. They should be the same length. Replace if needed. Repeat this test for the rear springs.
6. Foam Tyres — Left and right tyres are not close to the same diameter. If the tyre diameter on the left front is significantly different to the right front (more than 0.4mm), or if the left rear is significantly different to the right rear, then this may be a contributing factor to an ill-handling car.

Lacking Acceleration or Started Oversteering

If the car was working well but is now lacking acceleration or has started oversteering then:

1. Check belts are not worn or slipping.
2. Check CVDs/DCJs are working properly and set screws haven't come loose/blades are not worn.
3. Check motor temperature (refer to page 129).
4. Ball differential may be slipping too much. Tighten using the recommendations on page 115.

Check out my other RC books and eBooks at www.davebstevens.com

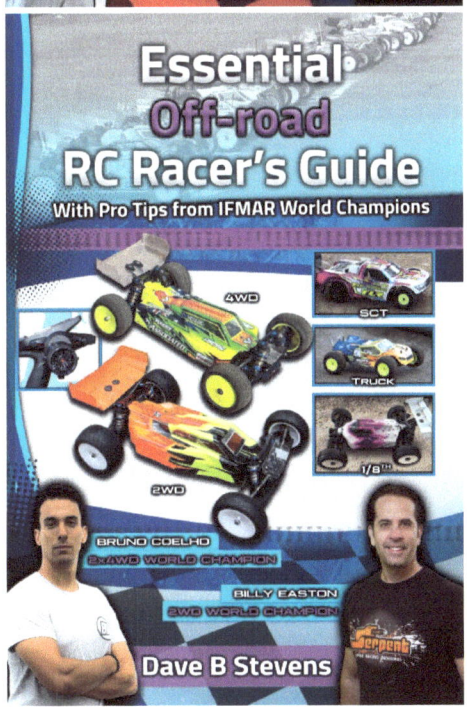

Quick Reference

Maintenance	250
After Run Checks	250
Between Events	251
Re-building a Car	252
Correcting Key Balance Issues	254
Traction – How to Increase	254
Steering	256
Too Much Steering (Oversteer)	256
Not Enough Steering (Understeer)	258
Steering Response Changes for No Apparent Reason	259
Traction Rolling	260
Easier to Drive – How To	261
Troubleshooting	262
Car Wanders on the Straight	262
Change of Direction (Chicane)	262
Fast Sweeper Cornering	262
Car 'Hops' or 'Chatters' Across the Track	262
Tyres Picking Up Carpet Debris from Track	262
Inconsistent Handling	263
Lacking Acceleration or Started Oversteering	263

www.ingramcontent.com/pod-product-compliance
Lightning Source LLC
Chambersburg PA
CBHW041459010526
44107CB00044B/1502